Hear Our Stories

Writings on Migration

Hear Our Stories

Writings on Migration

Editors

Teresa Norman, Sinéad Mangan-Mc Hale &
Consuelo Rivera-Fuentes

Typesetting and layout: Jorge Vasquez
Cover Artwork: @Sophie MacKenzie
Cover Design: Triona Walsh

British Library Cataloguing in Publication Data
A catalogue record for this book is available from the
British Library.
ISBN: 978-1-7395801-0-0

Typeset in 12pt Garamond
Printed and bound in Great Britain by 4edge Ltd

Cover illustration

The illustration on the cover is created by the artist, Sophie MacKenzie, based on a concept by Kosta Eleftheriadis. The artwork represents a play on the word anthology and the ancient Greek word for flower, Anthos.

The artist depicts the authors from this anthology watering a bed of flowers from where people are emerging to make the journey from their homeland. This is a metaphor to illustrate that, by sharing their stories, authors are helping others in similar situations to live, grow and blossom.

Dedication

Thank you to the many millions of migrants and refugees who leave their homes behind and make the hazardous and often lonely journey to build a new life. Our gratitude to those who generously share their stories in this anthology.

Foreword

I have always been passionate about encouraging and supporting inclusivity within the UK and so in 2016, I came up with the idea of creating TogetherintheUK (TGIUK) as an impartial non-profit making organisation. I was fortunate to be joined by three other like-minded individuals, and together we have developed an unbiased communications platform for migrants and refugees to safely share their stories, and to provide reliable advice and insights into life in the United Kingdom.

We wanted to open the minds and hearts of citizens in this country and encourage them to welcome new and diverse people to their community. Since then, we have been privileged to share many individual stories detailing the complexities of migration. At the core of each of these stories is a sense of courage, determination, and hope. We are always developing deeper insight into what it means to leave your country and start again. We post migrant stories in blogs, interviews, and podcasts across our social media channels. We also provide information sources for navigating the often complex and lengthy processes necessary to live and work in the UK.

In 2021, during what we hope will be the worst and last global pandemic in our lifetime, I felt that this was the perfect time for connection through the sharing of stories and so created our first Storytelling competition. We were delighted with the number of entries in the form of poems, short stories, and essays. The writers, some writing under pseudonyms, are both first and second-generation migrants and come from a range of different backgrounds, cultures, ages, gender, and experiences, each with their own unique story to tell.

For many of the writers in this anthology, English is not their first language and yet they have found a beautiful way to share their insights and transform their experience into art. We hope that this book will help you gain a deeper insight into the joys and sorrows of migration. We have left much of their writing as we received it, as we know readers want to hear the true voice of the writers. TGIUK have been greatly assisted by the professional and sensitive editing of Consuelo Rivera-Fuentes and Sinéad Mangan-Mc Hale.

I wanted to share a coherent migration story and so we set out the anthology in distinct chapters to represent the different stages migrants face when coming to the United Kingdom. These stages go from making the journey, to waiting for a visa to be granted, facing discrimination along the way, to making a new home in the UK. Our final chapter looks at the re-connection with the country of origin as being a migrant means having a relationship with two cultures in two different countries.

I hope that you enjoy reading these stories as much as we did. The anthology is a tribute to every person who has made a new home in the UK and honours those who have embraced and welcomed them. Stories help us connect with each other and we hope you connect with the writers and with the mission of TGIUK.

Teresa Norman
Co-founder and CEO of TogetherintheUK

Acknowledgements

A huge thank you to the many people who helped with the production of *Hear Our Stories*. Their support has meant that through this book we are able to create a platform to tell the important stories of migrants and refugees. We are forever grateful for their continued support.

It would be impossible to thank everybody in person, but there are some people without whom we would not be able to publish this anthology. Firstly, thank you to the wonderful writers for sharing their creativity and their moving personal stories with us. We are very proud to share their words with you.

Secondly and very importantly, we would like to acknowledge the time and efforts invested by the judges of the Storytelling competition, Lord Dubs, Tyrone Roach, David Marshall, Jonathan Portes, Sunder Katwala, Consuelo Rivera-Fuentes, and Nazek Ramadan. They had a very difficult job! Our gratitude also goes to Lord Dubs, Nazek Ramadan, Jonathan Portes, Anna Pincus and Dr Alexandra Bulat for writing the introduction to each of our anthology chapters.

To Sophie MacKenzie, who, based on a concept by Kosta Eleftheriadis, created the beautiful illustration that covers this anthology. TGIUK would also like to thank Union Chapel Church for hosting the Storytelling competition award ceremony.

An exceptional acknowledgement must go to Consuelo Rivera-Fuentes, the chief editor and managing director of Victorina Press. Thanks also to Jorge Vasquez, Sophie Lloyd-Owen and all the staff at Victorina Press, who helped TGIUK through the process of publishing this anthology. We would not be here without their support and commitment to helping us share these stories.

And finally, to all the fantastic TGIUK volunteers, past and present, who have shared their time, expertise, and skill to make TogetherintheUK the positive presence it is to our community and society. We are indebted to you all and wish you happiness and health in your future.

Teresa Norman, Johann Taljaard, Kosta Eleftheriadis, Fatkma Bermeo Mustafa.
Co-founders of TogetherintheUK.

Table of Contents

INTRODUCTION TO THE ANTHOLOGY

Lord Alf Dubs

As an active refugee campaigner and having served for seven years as Refugee Council director, I was delighted and proud to be invited to preside over TogetherintheUK's (TGIUK) 2021 inaugural Storytelling competition.

My empathy and commitment to safeguarding refugees, particularly young children, comes from a very personal connection. I was one of the thousands of children fleeing the persecution of Jews in Nazi-occupied Czechoslovakia. I know that I, and many others, owe our lives to the persistent calls from refugee aid organisations and the opinions of the general British public who urged the government to help. My experience of arriving in a strange, foreign country at the age of six in 1939, influenced me greatly and helped shape my future. I have dedicated my life to channelling that great British humanitarian spirit to change immigration policies and processes. I firmly believe in the power of positive public opinion when it comes to campaigning on behalf of migrants and refugees who hope to enter the United Kingdom to either start a new life or reconnect with family already settled in our country.

A good story forges connections among people, a connection that is vital to our evolution. In 2020 and 2021, many of us endured the hardship of isolation and loneliness brought on by the COVID-19 pandemic. Listening to the stories of how people lived and died during that time strengthened our need for human connection and increased our compassion for others. Migrant stories take the reader one step further by sharing different cultures, traditions, and values. Through the words of migrants, we have the opportunity to see a

1

life outside of our own, to see how we all have the same desire to live a happy and safe life despite differences.

I know that my story of arriving in the United Kingdom as a child refugee connects me on a personal level with the British public and centres my strong held belief in the cause of refugees. As such, I firmly believe that it is only through hearing the personal stories of migrants that public opinion will become more inclusive and empathetic. These stories, often harrowing and heart-breaking, are also uplifting and motivational and can help people open their minds and hearts to migrants. I have always found that real-life stories provide us with an opportunity to learn from another person's experience, strengthening or challenging our opinions and values.

I know that this belief in the power of storytelling drives TGIUK to reach out to migrants, encouraging them to share their stories and why so many submitted entries to the TGIUK Storytelling competition. I enjoyed reading every one of the entries, and I firmly believe that the value of each of these stories was not in whether they won a prize or not, but in the fact that the writers shared insights about themselves and their individual experiences coming to the United Kingdom. They allowed us, as the reader, to see through the eyes of the storyteller, to become part of their story, and understand what it means to leave home and start a new life in a strange country.

For me, a good story does not tell us how to think but rather gives us questions to make us think. This is what these TGIUK stories have achieved.

CHAPTER 1 - THE JOURNEY

Lord Alf Dubs

Alf Dubs is a British Labour politician and former Member of Parliament. He has served two terms in the House of Commons and has a life peerage in the House of Lords. He is acknowledged as a stalwart supporter of refugees and has fought all his political life to improve the processing of refugees, particularly children, into the United Kingdom.

Introducing this chapter – The Journey – is a bittersweet experience for me. The stories and poems resonate with me on a very personal level as I recall my own experiences as a child leaving my family to escape the Nazi persecution of Jews in Czechoslovakia. My journey, as part of a British led Kindertransport, was difficult, of course, but the actual train journey was relatively easy and comfortable. When I read these harrowing stories, I once again am grateful for the people of the United Kingdom who made the journey of so many children possible and who welcomed us into their country.

The stories below will give you just some insight into the harsh conditions that far too many migrants and refugees endure. We should never forget that for many, making that journey means losing almost everything of the life they had, family and friends; that alone is a traumatic experience. These personal accounts tell of the evil of people taking advantage of the desperate but also show the kindness of strangers offering comfort along the journey. As one of our young writers so succinctly wrote, "what I would give to be in a safe place".

3

While many survive the terrible experiences that led them to flee, enduring the treacherous journey to reach the United Kingdom, for some, just surviving has become their new challenge. I hope that by reading these journey stories, you will have a greater understanding of the challenges migrants and refugees face and open your hearts to be kind and welcoming.

Sipwe's Journey Begins

Johann

Johann is originally from South Africa and is a co-founder of TogetherintheUK. His story sets out that when we migrate, we cannot know what we will find. We know, for instance, that many migrants think that they will come to the UK for just a short time and then in a heartbeat, twenty years go by, and the UK is their journey's end.

Sipwe, a young man in his early twenties, living in a small village in the foothills of the mighty Drakensberg Mountain range in Southern Africa, is very pensive as he walks the 15 km to the nearest 'big' town. He is going to see the wise old man sitting in the square under the "iNdaba" tree.

This has been the place, under the iNdaba tree, where for eons the elders of the villages would meet and discuss and resolve communal issues and disputes. Meetings could sometimes go on for days and always accompanied by copious calabashes of sorghum beer, an alcoholic drink made from fermented maize.

Sipwe had a burning question that he needed an answer to. Sipwe had been a very thoughtful but restless boy, even more evident now that he is a young man. He is always searching for higher meaning in his, and the lives of his family. He is not exactly sure what he is looking for, but he feels it all the time. All his actions and thoughts are driven by this search within himself. It has at times brought him into conflict with his traditional father and other elders in the village.

His father Sipho, a wise man himself, often suggested to Sipwe that life is a journey. A journey that every man, woman, and their children undertake until death comes and lays one to rest. Sipwe then asked on numerous occasions "How long is the journey, what is the destination and when will I get there?", to which Sipho always replied "You will know when you get there". Sipwe found this very confusing. "How can you go somewhere if you don't know where to go? How do you know how long it will take, what to take with you for the journey? How will you know when and if you have arrived?" To which Sipho just warmly says, "Sipwe, you will know all the answers when you get there".

Finally, Sipwe decided to go and speak with Dinganiwa, the wise old man. Tentatively he approached Dinganiwa sitting on an exposed large root of the iNdaba tree.

"Molo, baba Dinganiwa, kunjani we?" "Molo umfaniwe, I am well and you too.

"Shala pansi (sit down) and let us talk."
Nervously Sipwe sat down and looked at Dinganiwa and says:

"Dinganiwa, I come for your help. I want to know why my father always tells me that life is a journey and even though the destination is not known, I will know when I get there, how I got there and why I ended up there?"

Dinganiwa says very softly: "Issh ", an expression indicating "I need to think about this for a moment" accompanied by a shaking head.

"Sipwe, I think your father is right! He is teaching you well and you will become a strong man amongst other men. Sipho is right about the most important lesson, which is you will know all the answers when you get there! I think you have to go on your journey now, leave the village, look towards the distance and start your journey."

Sipwe felt dismayed and said: "I have not received any answer or wisdom today, and the question is still the same. How will I know my destination?" To this Dinganiwa just replied: "Sipwe, he who knows the destination never learns the way. And for you dear Sipwe, he who knows not one thing, knows another".

Finally, Sipwe started to understand and decided to tackle his journey free of doubt!

TGIUK

My Eritrea

Daniel Habte

This poem depicts the treacherous journey made
by Daniel, as a child, from Eritrea to England.
He shares tales of cruelty and kindness along his
odyssey. While safe and loved with a new family,
Daniel still misses his mother.

This is my story …
My Eritrea, it is a beautiful, blessed yet brutal land.
You can work hard to make a success of your life,
but you have no control to decide where you stand!
The fear of a life held captive by hard, cruel leaders,
living in the dirt, rubbed deep in my hurt of missing my
family and friends.
Do I stay and carry out the military demand?

At the age of 14 and the idea of leaving all this for …
the unknown actually seemed like the better plan.
For girls, it's bad, made to marry young to an old man.
Forced out of education into life detention. This is not
the life, Dan, this is not the life.

I could see the border from where I lived, it looked so
appealing.
Seeing countless failed escape attempts, "I could do it!"
– was my gut feeling.
With nothing but the clothes I was wearing,
no family to express my leaving, but not for lack of
caring,
just because they couldn't bear it, to know that I was
absent.

I had to be so careful, always checking over my shoulder,
I was alone and scared, but the adrenaline pushed me to
be bolder!
I had made it, but it wasn't over.
Walking for two days across the desert, through the
forests,
fearing for my life in the darkness as I heard the
unnerving noises of a hyena's chorus.
I felt so alone.

Three weeks later, captured in Ethiopia, seeking refuge
in camp Endabanguna.
The next week, at Camp Adi Harish, a kind woman
from my village recognised my face.
She took me as her son, insisting that I belong alongside
her suitcase.

We were there for two months, some people much
longer.
I can still remember the body aching tiredness, along
with the hunger.
But we knew we had to move on. Move on.
Finding transport to our next journey, Sudan.

The woman took out her coins and paid a man.
Her kindness that day I'll never repay, as in a moment
... she was gone.
Travelling across the Sahara, on a truck ram packed with
people,
packed like sardines, legs hanging out, feeling crushed
like a beetle.

Hanging off the truck driving so fast, some fell, too late.
No going back now, that's the end for them, the desert
is their fate.

There's nothing we could do.
It could be one of us next, this is all we knew.

Arrived in Libya, after a journey that only my God could save me from,
was held for a month, in a hall amongst 2,000 other migrants.
One loo, little food, no shower, a drip of water. Barely enough to live.
Bugs crawling in our dirt and over our bodies, what I'd give to be in a safe place.
Somewhere clean.
This was what I was striving for, this was the dream.

I have never witnessed or experienced cruelty like this, I did not feel human.
If we were seen speaking to anyone, we could be beaten, or even killed.
I won't mention the ways that I have seen this happen, you would feel so ill.

Finally, an answer to a prayer, my cousin raised $2,000 for me to leave.
I'm taken to a boat where I could float across to Italy.
On the boat, another vessel for too many people, trying desperately to escape their lives.
Women on the top deck, men down below.
People fainting, covered in vomit head to toe.
There was some food going around, but the women needed it first.
It wouldn't be too long now before the first man dies of thirst.

I could hear that everyone on the deck was shouting that we were going the wrong way, others instructing everyone that we needed to pray, everyone had to pray!

Italian authorities found us stranded out at sea.
They pulled us across like limp fish quivering at the knees.
People half dead due to the conditions, hunger, and the heat.
We were taken somewhere by vehicles and then just dumped out on the street.

I made my way to the train station and travelled across to Calais in France,
that is where everyone was heading, where we were told we had a chance.
I managed to stay for only a few days, others had made up their homes,
as if the long journey had conquered them and they'd accepted their slum kingdom.

I was snuck onto a lorry with eight other strangers, this was our chance to escape.
We had to endure another journey; this time trapped between two large crates.
We were fighting for our survival, no air to barely breathe,
banging furiously on the walls, for our helpless bodies beneath.
The lorry had boarded a ship to the UK, we were almost there.

Out on the other side, the police had found us, and to cut a long story short,
I'm escorted to a holding room and then taken by police transport.

My nerves are racing but I am holding on to hope.
My God has helped me thus far and given me the strength to cope.

The county foster services took over because I was still considered a child.
Despite this journey making me a man, I am reminded that I am still a child.
When I first met my English foster parents, I could not trust them.
Because the people I had met along my way had made me question people.

It took time to relax in my new home.
But I quickly learnt that my new family did care for me, they treated me like a son.
Life is challenging,
knowing that I still have family in Eritrea
and that I haven't seen my mum in a long time.
But I praise God for getting me through this journey because
He was always watching over me.
Always guiding my path.

TGIUK

Survivor's Plea

Michael Ndoun

Michael composed a series of three poems to reflect the struggles of immigrants. Through his words he conveys the mental and physical trauma that so many face in their journey to a safer environment. In his poems he discusses and demonstrates the struggles of a troubled man who has been destroyed in the pursuit of freedom. It reflects a level of naivety for believing he would be protected by the same organisation that ultimately destroyed him.

Picture your average victim of torture.
Appears confident, purposeful and
competent
but masked by pain and treachery.
Beneath the surface (which is in itself
another journey),
you will find a broken, lost
and fragile individual on the verge
of giving up.

In suffering, I hide those voices that cry in pain.
The agonising pain was
gold dust in the hands of the Gods
of torment.
In his long reach, my life was
shattered.
In his presence, my destiny
altered.

I dreamt I was amongst the ones
that drowned till death.

I tried to halt my breath even though the truth couldn't
unravel me after death.
For once in my life, I was scared of death.
I pleaded, give me death but don't
just put me in the fire with rest.
They replied, the night's still young, so confront your
death.
In death, I scuffle my despondent pain,
to confront this romantic euthanasia strain.
Though it awakes my heart but delights it with esoteric
pain.

This same flower that smiles today,
now dying in shame.
A sorrowful song of death playing in the background
hoping
for the living to listen to the call
of agony.
Singing by the darkened clouds,
dying by the moonlight rise.
Changing from the gloomy night
to a morning rise.
Little gentle music singing,
shadows on shadows, whilst dancing
and smiling to the bliss of dying.

From the home of the struggling
and suffering,
the pain seems so glistening though
it's devouring.
Out in a world of death, far from
the mellow springs of life, so pouring.
Underneath the sun and the moon,
life is still nursing.
Underneath the dusk and the day,

life is still changing.
Underneath the glimmering of stars and the grandeur
of the sunsets,
hope is rising.
I trust the world won't see me crying,
even though I'm dying.

I'm dying! I'm dying!
Fear of slowly dying has consumed
my will of living.
I won't waste today's chance of living
just to crying, reaching, and dying.
I'm tired of trying, I want to experience some living,
enough of the dying.
No more dying. No more fighting.
Bullets of fear are flying,
whilst dreams are dying.

See the tears of the angels looking down on me crying.
Life is falling away from my grasp but still fighting.
Gone through living just for dying.
Gone through laughing just for living.
Gone through living just for crying.
Waiting for the sun, a chance at a new day.
Worth living.

TGIUK

The Journey (1964)

Abida Akram

Abida was born in the Punjab in Pakistan. She came to England with her mother and sister to join her father, whom she had never met, in the mid-1960s. The trauma of leaving her beloved extended family behind was huge. The bewildering journey, lack of English, and the first few lonely cold years in England are forever etched in her memory. And it is these memories of being an immigrant that inspired her writing. Abida is proud of being an immigrant and doing well in a country that does not always make it easy to belong or to be successful.

Fear fogged my mind
as we leave the ground,
tied up in the belly of
a roaring, whining metal bird.
Blood rushing in my ears,
my heart beating fast with the roar.

A fog, damp and metal-grey.
Tall pale faces walking by, like
ghost balloons with pale hands.
Terrified, I clutch the black, soft folds of
mother's burka.

Shivering in thin cotton, orange shalwar kameez,
I ask her in Punjabi,
'Ameeji, Victoria qui heh?'
This word, repeated,
bounced off the vast ceiling.
Was this loud, tinny noise – God?

Only the racket of trains,
a familiar soundtrack from back home.

Not yet four years old,
I hid in mother's folds.
A still black triangle
in an ocean of sound and a crowd of
strangely dressed people.
Waiting for a father I had never known.

I must have been bad,
to make the world lose its colour.
Where had the sun gone?
A cacophony of grey sounds,
with strangers who did not smile,
eyes that skimmed over me.

Melting, cold pieces
of soft cotton falling from a slate-grey sky,
three months later,
made me laugh with wonder.

A year later, I found my voice again.

Human Smuggling

Yousef

As a refugee fleeing a war-stricken country, Yousef conveys through his heartfelt words, the exploitation and cruelty that is experienced by so many refugees in their struggle to find a better life. The key message in this piece is the exploitation of vulnerable people. To ensure that this message is clearly understood, TGIUK has slightly edited some of the wording, but the voice and the depth of the message remains Yousef's.

I am one of the many people who have fled their country, searching for peace, tranquillity, and the chance of a real life. My country has been ravaged by the cruelty of the Darfur government and the militia group, the Janjaweed. Living there was rough and disgusting and I had to flee, becoming homeless in neighbouring countries. The story of my escape is brutal, but it is true and without exaggeration.

My journey began in North Darfur and on to Libya. I travelled by car from North Darfur through the harsh desert, enduring the most difficult days of my life. Along with other refugees, I travelled for 21 days in the car. The car broke down and we had to spend 17 days in the desert with barely any water. We were victim of human smuggling gangs. Gangs that offer the "desperate" the chance to escape but who treat us cruelly. To these people, refugees in search of salvation are just cheap commodities, treated disgustingly, smuggled in miserable means of transport, shipped alongside animals.

It is important that people recognise the

exploitation that refugees are subjected to. It is not just the physical cruelty and hardship of fleeing their country and reaching the UK. Refugees not only have to pay an exorbitant amount of money to make the journey but then many are blackmailed once they arrive. The level of extortion is so strong and so violent; these people do not see us as humans but rather as a wasteful commodity which can be disposed of without a second thought.

This is not a story; it continues day in and day out.

PTSD, the Ripple Effect, Again and Again

Asha

Asha immigrated from the Caribbean to the UK in 2010. She is keen to share the trauma of migrants to shed some light on the challenges they face.

I relive my pain every day,
every quiet moment again and again and again,
it comes to haunt me.
I lie in my bed wide awake because I am stuck in a dream
I can't escape.
As my scary thoughts just grows bigger, my memories
now come rushing back.
All my conscience just goes black,
I scream within myself.
The tears I can't hold back just trickle down with my
internal pain.
At times, I feel so ashamed it comes to haunt me again
and again.
I sit up and wonder what it truly feels to be happy,
to smile once without faking,
to not just want to cry all the time,
to know what is like to be hopeful,
to live in the now and not in the past, again and again.
To have a future dream,
to see myself happy and be truly happy and not just like
a blank screen,
to have someone who understands me,
to be free from my own mind,
to not have this pain I carry every day,
again and again.

TGIUK

Inevitability

Mika

Mika, originally from Azerbaijan, has been in the UK for more than five years. When writing this poem, she was inspired by a story told by a friend. This version of her story reminds her how scary it can be when in a new place facing struggle and change. Over the years though, Mika has learnt that at the end of the day we are all going to be fine and that it is okay to be scared. It is important to be strong to survive and this is even more important for people who are far away from their hometown.

Time and circumstances
turn the soul of a dreamy natured child into a resilient warrior.
From a little surprised girl,
she turned into a person
who soberly assesses the priorities of life
and chooses for herself a difficult path to self-affirmation.

Miss L was naive and dreamy.
Her future was bright.
But life is cruel.
She understood this later.

Miss L looks towards the night sky
and hopes her father and mother have a place in heaven.

Life went on,
happiness,

sadness,
hunger,
resentment.

She believed that one day things will be better again,
as they were in her childhood days.

Miss L must move to a safer place.
She cried inside of her heart.

The problem didn't end when she reached new shores.
She finds she must continue fighting.
But she is resolute.

The time is now,
she keeps her faith.
Betrayal, suffering, the battles are endless.
They tried to turn her into a monster
but she didn't let them break her.
She'd rather be the warrior girl.

She is far away from her hometown.
But after all her experiences,
she is still here,
she is still alive.
Miss L will fight until the very end.
It is inevitable.

Even Rain has an Identity

Morshed Akhtar

Morshed Akhtar emigrated from Dhaka in Bangladesh at a mature age. He left his beloved country, friends, and families behind, but brought a wealth of memories with him. He is never bored as he can see art in everything, and it is that art that motivates him. Morshed wrote this poem to show that while migrant communities all over the world share collective pain, experienced through their life journeys, each will experience this pain differently.

It was raining this morning
early morning -
very early and wakes me up in this morning,
the morning rains.
Tap on the window with a piece of sound
it's not making a classical note of the Bilabol, Voirobee,
not even the Jhumoor*
– that I know for long.
Still,
I'm early in the morning.
It wakes me up earlier than usual.
It keeps me awake and … and doesn't let me go back to sleep.
Cannot go back to sleep even I tried hard.

I have yet to get to know this foreign rain.
Hah! Foreign rain! Remains unknown!
So, this rain remains foreign to me with a strong identity.
So, even rains have an identity, do they?
What is my identity then, in this land?
But does the rain also have a race?

Which race do I belong to?
Do they have a citizen format?

I don't know, I lost my understanding.
I'm so worried. I still stay awake, wet
– wet inside.
I am in this land for long, and they still say it's not mine!
It's raining!
Am I a stranger, yet untuned!
Still!

* Bilawal, Voirobee, Jhomoor are raga and the basis for the eponymous musical mode in Indian classical music

Banksy

Narjes Azimi

Narjes Azimi is a poet and author. Her family
are originally from Iran. She is very aware of the
narratives and stories of conflict zones and writes
for the purpose of cosmopolitan peace. She writes
in English although English is her fourth language.
She has a PhD in Communication and Media
Studies, but her focus is poetry and creative writing.
This poem was inspired by Banksy's artwork, she
loves his contradictory style and how he overlaps
sorrow with love and dreams. This poem could be
any child in his street art. Banksy artistically creates
them; Narjes asks them to speak out.

Banksy,
I am the girl, who vanished in the murky border,
in short biography of the happy girl, by Narjes Azimi,
with the story of my brother in the darkest war ever.
Hi Banksy, I heard a lot about you!
Maybe you saw us over there,
with those shrewd eyes you have,
how pretty you painted us, our misery!
You cancelled it; how did you know
our dreams no longer exist?
Man, you know how we feel!
Your eyes watching us wisely.
How our souls evaporate in that gloomy night?
How our little hands could just cut our own skin, not a
barbed wire?
Thanks for painting us,
thanks for thinking about us,
thanks for watching us.

Our paper tops were our only property,
we ornamented the barbed wire.
The trees another side of the border calling us,
with their ripe apples waving to us.
Oh, again apples, apple tree,
even now, even for children, even in war,
apples seduced us again.
We took them with our red hands
and they took us bloody handed
in the cold autumn, our heart gone with the breeze.
Paper tops remained in rustling leaves,
without spinning again.

Received

Jaimin

Jaimin was born in the UK and his heritage is English and Indian on his mother's side. His mother was born in Kenya and her family origin is from Gujarat. He wrote this poem in response to the refugee crisis.

Bodies wash up on our shores,
on the golden sands, whose warm blood the sea stole.
Vessels, vessels, by which they tried to come,
and to which they turned. Crammed beyond measure,
and empty beyond.

Bodies wash up on our shores,
mouths to feed, and problems of our own. I know, I
know.
To ignore our own pain, is not a step in which we gain.

Bodies wash up on our shores,
again, but then, again, once a foot is set on our soil,
sand, and dirt,
once a mouth feeds off our bread, once a hand takes to
our work,
there is no reason under our sun, to say that it is still
they,
they, that have come, they, that are here.
So, when them and they, who turn to us and into we,
not as a nation, not as a country,
an island of people,
then what is there, that we cannot make our strength.
So, receive, receive we must, receive we will.
For no other sake, nor any other reason,
than to not let drown, any more good will.

TGIUK

The Channel

Kisa

Kisa wrote this to convey the desperation and determination that enables refugees to take the most dangerous of journeys. At the same time, it teaches us that we must continue to dream and to think beyond the problems we currently face, to look and find a better place.

I can't swim
but still, we swim away,
through choppy waters, colder than I've known,
far away from the ivory and oil,
from the machetes and men of blood.

I was born dusty as the floor beneath my mother's bed.
Many men had her there.
And I hated them.
But she taught me to look beyond our walls,
beyond the cutting hours, and to reach through the dark
into the light, to other lands.

So, my grip is tight
and my sight is set on fat green fields,
on warm people and cities of gold and glass.
I swim forwards, arm over tired arm,
to dream to arrive,
but the water is cold.

TGIUK

CHAPTER 2 - GETTING GRANTED

Anna Pincus

Anna Pincus, a founder and co-ordinator of Refugee Tales, has worked as a director of Gatwick Detainees Welfare Group (GDWG) for over ten years supporting people held in immigration detention and the volunteers who visit them weekly, managing outreach work and raising awareness about the campaign to end indefinite detention.

'The difference between you and me is a passport'

I am delighted to be asked to introduce this chapter of the TogetherintheUK anthology. The title, 'Getting Granted', is a phrase picked up from someone waiting to discover whether they will be granted 'refugee status' or 'the right to remain'. Without these being granted, people that come to the UK claiming asylum are denied the rights that citizens enjoy, such as the right to work. Asylum seekers are not allowed to work and at the time of writing, are given a cash allowance of £37.75 a week. This chapter is about the human cost of being held in this limbo. Being denied the dignity of work as well as respect, both from yourself and others, when you support yourself financially. It is a suspended life. The writings in this chapter reflect some of these events and emotions.

Without being granted 'status', people may end up in immigration removal centres and sent back to a country that they have fled, on a removal or deportation flight. Being held in detention with no time limit has a profound impact on the mental health of those that are detained that continues long after physical detention is over. Prisoners that are in the criminal justice system count down the days to the end of their sentence but people that are indefinitely detained in the UK, 'count up' the days to an uncertain future. Refugee Tales calls for a future without detention and seeks to honour the stories of those that have been detained and are living in limbo.

Like TGIUK, Refugee Tales provides a voice for refugees. We share the stories of people that have been held in indefinite immigration detention, and the tales of those who work with them. Some of the tales are first-hand accounts, whilst others are collaborations between people that have experienced detention and celebrated poets, novelists and writers. Refugee Tales is rooted in the work of Gatwick Detainees Welfare Group, a charity that supports people both held in immigration detention and on release from detention as people that have been detained often face destitution on release.

The Hostel

Frank

Frank is originally from Uganda and came to the UK in 2018 to achieve his dreams. Frank uses the character in this piece to show the reader that we all have differences and that we should respect and accept each other. He believes it is important for 'travellers' to tell their stories.

It's always hard having to leave home, but we do it to steer our lives to achieve the dreams we have. I thought this was a chance to get away, but it felt like it was the same story just repeated. I thought this time I was sure of safety. A thousand wrongs done, couldn't outweigh the benefit of this country sheltering me.

My very last days in the assigned hostel based in Edgewell, reminded me of the time when I left home the first time, and once again I felt unsafe. I knew I had to leave. But thanks to Alex, a friend I met in a social group, who let me stay with him for three nights and days, I slept so well, never have I slept from 8pm at night until 8am in the morning — it was amazing. My first morning, I felt so fresh and brand new, confident of a bright beginning, though I was still anxious of my decision to leave the hostel. The only thing that kept me going was Alex, my guardian angel, who watched my every step and guided my every move.

Waiting for my application for refugee status approval was like waiting for rain to fall in the Sahara. It felt like an eternity waiting for a "YES". "Everything happens for a good reason" my nan used to say. And she was right as while I was at the Home Office department waiting, I met a young friend called 'Happy'. Her questions and conversations brightened me and lightened my waiting. But worrying never leaves us, always worrying about the unknown. Driving home with my guardian angel, my phone rang. I picked up and heard the voice on the other side saying, "your application has been accepted". This delighted us but then we remembered to ask about my college and tuition applications, and they were all 'Yes' too!". I let out a sigh of relief, just like the day when I stepped onto the airplane, running away from the "righteous".

My guardian angel drove me straight to Safe Harbour Hostel. Right away I was given a room, sharing it with another migrant, another traveller. I felt so happy, like I was on top of a mountain looking down at the city. The hostel was more like a hotel, and I was a welcomed traveller eating and sleeping, like everyone else. In my mind, it still seemed unbelievable – I had made it out again.

All of us travellers in the hostel had the same stories. Just looking at some of them, I could tell what was in their minds. A sigh of relief and the feeling of being born again and escaping the past. Though I was not sure from what they were escaping, but I could sense the similarities and the hope in almost all of us. Many were grateful, though some wanted more. However, for me, it was a mission accomplished, a war won, and a test passed.

Rooms at the hostel were shared by two to four travellers waiting to be given a permanent home, making the hostel a temporary accommodation. There was no criteria for moving, some could be moved within days, weeks, or even months. While we waited, we all prayed and wished for the same in life; to be accepted and freed. Some people were brave enough and would share their stories but not everyone.

The luckiest migrants were those who had other travellers in the hostel with the same religion and the same language. However, despite similarities and all being refugees and asylum seekers in the same circumstances, we still had our differences, and many lived in fear of expressing who they were, and risking being rejected by their own kind because of arrogance and selfishness. We had all survived leaving our homes and making the difficult journey to a new country and a different culture, unsure of what to find but with faith and hope to find freedom. One would think this similarity would bond all travellers, but prejudice and discriminations remains within us all. Too many travellers failed to accept and embrace our differences but still stuck within their own understandings. A small group of these travellers were LGBTQ, something unacceptable for some people in the hostel, despite their holy book branding them as peaceful and loving people. One traveller, when with his own community was the stereotypical homophobe, but was in fact gay and still in the closet. To me, it was hypocritical, but understandable.

For many of the travellers, having so much free time with nothing to do was depressing. Some dreamed of having money to buy "nice" things. This desire, lead some doing things that they would not have dared do any other place. For Adam, male prostitution bailed him out. He asked if I, an athletic man, was up for the job. Apparently, we have "the energy" to work, - "only two hours and you can be smiling with money." It was not the choice for me.

Travellers from places such as the Middle East, Asia, and Africa, crossed borders on boats over oceans looking for freedom and safety from places they have never been before. For many, our past makes us stronger, but for some it can be a different story. Rabat, an honest and good man, still lives in fear and the memory of witnessing his family being executed made him broken, not stronger.

Travellers often feel exploited, particularly when help given is made feel like a favour and a debt. In many cultures, elders are highly respected and cannot be questioned and when they offer "help or a favour", to young travellers, it must be accepted. And so, some travellers are promised good jobs and houses, but the reality is they are being kept in other people's houses with no payment and no freedom. Many are treated as machines and expected to deliver the best and to live a life of a slave.

Safe Harbour hostel taught me a lot of life lessons and prepared me for the outside world. The many differences of language, religion, culture, opinions, and attitudes amongst the travellers reflected the nature of the world outside the hostel. While we waited, we all prayed and wished for the same in life; to be accepted and freed. It is hard for travellers to live alone, without their natural community, and many need to be helped to make the adjustment. Some people were brave enough to share their stories but not everyone.

I understand the reasons for the many Home Office interviews, and the questions they ask to determine your status, but these people and their questions push travellers back into their fears, into memories they do not want to remember. Some decide to bury all their thoughts and fears into being busy and not talking about their past experiences.

But travellers need to tell their stories.

My Life Story

Chelsy George

Chelsy's piece gives the readers insight, through the eyes of a child, the disruptive life migrants and their families endure as they await being legally accepted in the UK. Chelsy describes the challenges of moving from location to location, starting new schools and making and leaving friends. She overcame these challenges and wants her story to inspire other children facing similar circumstances to stay strong.

My life has had many ups and downs; a bumpy road that can lead to insecurity and uncertainty. There are times you will question whether you just do not fit in to today's "society" or people just do not understand you for who you are. A long journey to fight for your rights will always have obstacles. These obstacles build you up for what you can be in the future.

When I was a young child, everything seemed so perfect. I was in my own bubble. Life seemed perfect. Then we moved. Being the young child I was, I did not feel that there was any issue. My mom and I just moving to another city – what was the big deal?

Me being a curious and inquisitive child, I was able to quickly adjust to my new surroundings. Everything seemed to go back to normal – nothing seemed to be the matter. Before I knew it, we moved again. On the road, looking at the sky turn to candyfloss, waiting to reach your "home". A room was what I would call home. Didn't realise that it was going to be the continuous pattern for the next five years or so.

Well, guess what? We moved … again. Moved to a new city. I began my primary education in this city.

I began to fall in love with this city. People were so kind and generous. I had loads of friends. Then they threatened to take that all away from me. And they did. From friends I thought I would have until the end. Gone. Just because me being in the country that they believe belongs to them. The country that I was born in and had lived in my entire life was not enough for me to claim that it was also mine.

The whole process of finding me a new school was another hassle. The only school was two bus journeys away, meaning the journey was always a very long one. But I always had a love for school, so I always looked at the positive of having the privilege of learning. I also made my first ever best friend. She was going to be my friend forever, even though we had barely known each other for a week. We would only play with each other, and we liked it that way. It was fun! Then, we had to be parted from each other, because of them. The people who just want you to feel miserable.

In 2014, I came to Birmingham; this city seemed very big with lots of people. Then I met two people who I was going to forever consider as family. My time in Birmingham was where I was going to grow up and become more knowledgeable about the system and life. I lived in various accommodations that ranged from being okay to being absolutely rubbish! The worst I lived in was a flat in Aston. When you looked at the outside it looked very posh, quite sophisticated, and clean. However, once you were inside the building it was a completely different place. A place that the Social Services thought was a suitable environment for a child to grow up in. Where people would fight and do the most terrible things. Where people would steal things. So much for wanting children to grow up in places that are "safe and "nurturing".

When I mentioned stealing, it had happened to me. I had this bike that I was trying to learn how to ride, but we could not keep it inside the flat, because there just wasn't enough space to put it. So, we had to keep it outside the door. One day, we were going out and then we realised it was no longer there. We asked people there if they had seen it, but no-one had seen it. My mum filed a report to the police, and we waited for a response. There was no reply until my mum had to call them herself: they told her that the case was closed, because it wasn't worth prosecuting. I always thought that the police were there to help you when you needed them. But in my case, they didn't want to help. How do you think a 7-year-old child would feel? I just felt sadness and disappointment.

Finally, we left that terrible flat and moved into a house. For the first time in forever, I had my own room and I settled down in a primary school! And behold, we were granted our leave to remain in 2018. I was able to finish my primary education with great SAT results! I am now in Year 8 at school in Birmingham.

Well, my story was filled with ups and down, but I am happy with where I am now. Me looking back at myself grow up over the years just shows how much I have grown in age and wisdom.

I hope my story inspires lots of children who are in the same situation as I was. You are stronger than you know!

TGIUK

Second Gen Immigrant

Evelyn Bayerlein

Evelyn Bayerlein's father, who is German, moved to the UK in 1998 and her mother, who is from Uganda, came here in 2000. She is, what is termed, a second-generation immigrant and wrote this poem to showcase the reality of not having, what is considered, the perfect "British" genealogy.

Second gen immigrant
both parents from afar.
Born in a country I call home
but doesn't treat me as its own.
My mother from Uganda,
a land once colonised
by where I live now.
My father a German,
born and raised
after the Second World War,
but now an ally of
where I live now.
A swirl of
German and Uganda
living in the land
of the former empire.
British born and raised
studying for days and days
to get GCSEs and A-levels,
to be denied a passport four times.
Hoping and wishing
for that citizenship,
to be naturalised
into a country

I have lived in all my life.
The country whose buses
I get frustrated with,
the education system I battled.
For what,
to be marginalised,
stopped and searched,
underrepresented, underpaid,
underhelped, underestimated?
Hoops to jump,
feeling hopeless.
I don't know any other country.
If I wasn't seen as a citizen here
where would I be a citizen of?
Both parents are from afar.

We are Dying

Loraine Masiya Mponela

Loraine is an autodidact poet and explores the theme of migration from personal lived experiences of the UK asylum and immigration system. Loraine is originally from Malawi but currently lives in Coventry, England. She has recently published a collection of her poems, *I Was Not Born A Sad Poet*. Since 2016, Loraine has been in the leadership team of CARAG and the "#Statusnow4all" campaign since its inception in April 2020.

We are dying
in isolation, alone and forlorn,
with not much change,
with not much hope.
Even in death there is "they don't matter".
We are dying.
There is no inquest,
there is no investigation,
like a useless life has deservedly just gone
and no one needs to know.
We are dying.
Our trauma is always downplayed,
wars and bullets we witnessed,
and abuse flying towards us
have made us feel unworthy, unloved, and undeserving.
We are dying.
We leave behind orphaned children,
paralysed
by the meaninglessness of their own lives.
Everything about us, ignored.
We are dying.

The hand of oppression is heavy
but it needs not muscles
to lift it off.
Come out, shout!
We are dying.
Sing the names
of the deceased,
let the world know
that they too once walked
this earth.
Say their names,
remind the world
of lives cut short,
lives that mattered to us.
We are dying.
Beat the drums.
Drum the call with a siren, not to war
but to a new level of consciousness
that says we are humans too,
though the hostile environment says we are not.
That we sing in defiance and call for recognition,
that our lives matter, if not to anyone else, to us.
Break the silence!
We too are humans,
documented or not!
Spread the message
of love!
We are dying.
We are dying.
We are dying.

I Own Nothing

Loraine Masiya Mponela

This is the second of Loraine's poems which depicts the stage of the journey when a homeless charity gave her shelter. The phrase "breaks my peace" came from an online workshop facilitated by David Dykes from LYRICI ARTS in September 2021.

I have a roof above my head.
I am glad, but it belongs to someone else.
I have no bills, I am just an occupant,
a happy occupant.
I own nothing.
I don't have to pay anything.
I don't own this space.
I am happy,
but something really bothers me
and breaks my peace.
Where is home?
I have others paying for me,
like a child
I've to be looked after.
One day I shall hand back my room keys,
when my time is up.
Where do I go from here?
I get anxious and these thoughts
break my peace.
I once had a home, a house I could afford,
like the life I once had,
it's all gone.
Refugee I am, no job, no income, no hope.
I am grateful

for the hand of providence in my life.
But I fear yet another hand,
which at the stroke of a pen can take it all away, and just
like that
I own nothing.
This breaks my peace.
The biggest fear of all is that
I am not alone.
So many are in this loop and
this breaks my peace.

Uncontrollable

Veruschka Mbai

Veruschka Mbai is a young girl, originally from Namibia and currently settling in the UK. She has great hopes for her future and writing is one of her joys. Veruschka finds writing helps her mentally escape from her current situation and allows her to share insights into her life.

It is a closet, called the "world we fit in". Dark enough to hide you from the light found within. You are alone when you count your scars, but if the world calls, you are ready to mask. We are afraid to be God's light. Because the dark makes a good secret hiding spot and it feels comfy alright. So, we stay pretending Instagram is kicking…life is going well, I wish I could film it…

I'm partly Christian, while another half is sinning. I know God is okay with it if I pray only on Sunday to show my side of religious commitment. I'm made in God's image, but the mirror is my only opposition.

The world is calling, can I borrow your mirror with your reflection in it? My soul is conflicted by religion. Is it wrong if I stick with Jesus but at the same time I don't keep his commandments? Or perhaps the depth of fears in me distracts me from being me and obeying. I don't know maybe if I could write to them, everything would be okay, and momma and I would be together. How do I commence? "Dear migrant officers" or perhaps they discard the matter to be classified as migrant officers, what do I do?

I am not good with words but, oh well here we go. I write this letter to speak for our (receive) hearts I write it with tears in my eyes because, despite everything,

I know that it will not erase our fears and distress. I write this letter to remind us how beautiful it is when we love each other. Please receive it from the heart of a young immigrant girl in despair. I hope my letter paints a rainbow of pictures, and colours with little sweetness. Lives are forcibly lost to a stigma, that degrades and humiliates the exhalation of an immigrant child.

The silence was my only weapon of choice, but this time my pain refused to be silent. It hurts to see how much we tear at each other, just to protect the same rights we refused to preserve, yet we are made of the same flesh. I think of the time we had peace as a common desire. Indeed, momma no longer smiles, sadness rested on her cheeks. She pays attention to the passage of time because she knows that at any time a letter will come from immigration to remind her that she is a stranger in a strange nation.

Young immigrant, permanently hiding from what seems like the iron loses the spear. Young immigrant, longing for acceptance and happiness. But it seems like no one understands and cares. Between the world and me, I've built up a wall. A young vibrant immigrant simply trapped, a prisoner of despair.

I don't know what's going on here, too many versions, too many colours, too many shades. During the day I hide from the light and the sun. I saw children cry with pain that shouldn't be theirs, wondering why hope was late, whilst they were on time. Who says love and pain should always go hand in hand? If we want love to reign right here, why do we let our hearts beat backwards.

I wish I could forget … forget all the tears and pain. Forget all the hurt and shame. Forget all the things of my past. Because like most, they didn't last.

Invisible Heroes

Ruth

> Ruth wrote this essay to highlight the practical
> challenges that people who are undocumented face
> every day in the UK. Their situation was particularly
> difficult during the COVID-19 pandemic and the
> restrictions that were put in place. Ruth conveys how
> frightening it is for many people to seek the help that
> is available to everyone else. She wants everyone to
> be 'visible'.

Here we are in a country that we thought we could call
home, a place to accomplish our dreams and to work to
support our families back in our own countries. Many
of us chose to stay after our visas expired so we could
continue to work. But little did we know that doing that
is a wrong decision as it only makes matters worse. When
you are undocumented your choices are limited and you
cannot access help from the government or services, so
you end up doing exploitative and underpaid jobs.

It is difficult to get affordable accommodation
close to your job as rent is very high and your meagre
wages aren't sufficient to pay the rent. So, you end up
having to travel very far to find cheap houses in areas
where you can afford the rent. Then you must commute
on long journeys to get to work, and half of your wages
are spent on travelling costs. We are too scared to ask
our employers for a pay rise in case they tell us to leave.

During the height of the pandemic, your health
was also at risk because of COVID-19, and you were
also putting the health of others at risk by not staying
at home because you still had to carry on working to
survive. The world is finally dealing with the COVID-19

pandemic. Several vaccines have been identified and the government is rolling them out to every adult in the UK. There was a campaign for undocumented migrants to be eligible for the vaccine and the government agreed that everyone regardless of their status should have access without risk of deportation. However, despite this reassurance, a lot of migrants are scared to come forward to be vaccinated and so are still posing a health risk to the public. And during the lockdown if you had a live-in job, your employer was too scared to let you go out, even if it was just to get a little fresh air. They were afraid that you might catch COVID and infect them as well. You had to stay locked up in the house every day as if you were a prisoner, at the same time worrying about the problems of your own families back home who depend on you as the main breadwinner.

Then there is the problem of getting signed up to a GP. There is the challenge of feeling unable to change to a GP closer to where you live because of the fear that they will ask for ID and proof of address, and this will stop you from accessing the service at all. Being undocumented is very hard as it brings so many practical and legal challenges when all you are trying to do is earn money and look after your family back home. I think undocumented migrants are invisible heroes as they are the ones who suffer a lot in silence because they are too scared to speak out or ask for help. They are living in deplorable and overcrowded conditions where they share accommodation with lots of strangers, often ten people or more. And there is not just the unease of having to share just one toilet and one kitchen with some many strangers, but it meant it was impossible to social distance during the pandemic. But what can they do, they don't have a choice, so they just must continue living an invisible life?

There are solutions to helping migrants to live a visible life. Giving undocumented migrants Indefinite Leave to Remain will give them the security to be able to rent proper accommodation or own their own homes. It will give them access to legal jobs where they can work and pay tax and pay into a pension. They would be able to access NHS services and be treated by trained medical practitioners when a medical issue arises. Undocumented migrants often avoid seeking medical help as they know they cannot afford to pay for medicines, or they use unsafe ways to cure ailments.

I want to live in a world where all undocumented people can be free and be like everybody else, a world of equal rights and status. A world where everyone is visible.

TGIUK

Uncivilised

Michael Ndoun

This is the second part of a trilogy that Michael wrote to showcase the struggle of a troubled man who has been destroyed in the pursuit of freedom. It reflects a level of naivety for believing he would be protected by the same organisation that ultimately destroyed him.

You say I'm uncivilised because I chose to protect that which seems so commonly uncommon.
What a treasured pursuit in a strange escape, old culture dying miserably,
murdered by the introduction of a new culture, created by those who are afraid to be insecurely secure.

Amid this new age
only the uncivilised can civilise the uncircumcised.
Morale depletion has instilled
reductionist and materialist debouch,
championed by a new culture
that is seen as an invitation to feel our way in the ruinous perception of a Machiavellian mind,
unscrupulously dangerous as self-exaltation is celebrated,
unravelling times solemnise the failure of a civilised nation and
2020 can testify to this notion.

Some say this is a mirror that divulges our human imperfection.
Voices are breaking in silence,
whilst silence is being broken with voices.
This crumbling narrative is now consumed by some

voiceless nation,
where our values are defined by self-promotion,
still educated and uncivilised,
imprisoned, and hypnotised, by the same placebo of
freedom,
destroyed by madness and starving nakedness,
victimised, penalised and criticised
by the same culture that promised to
protect them but now dismissed and despised.

How can we not question
the questioner's questions?
Everything seemed to act just like a drug.
How can we reimagine ourselves in world so nakedly
painted with dirt?
Unmasking this moon, hidden behind
the mask is treachery to a masked generation,
where myth and dreams converge.
Rather than a fait accompli assertion
we can see our fate without its mask.

The uncivilised are
holding vessel for multiple voices,
beauty is it truth, truth is it beauty?
In suffering, we lose ourselves to true human values.

Life was complicatedly distorted,
my best was badly reported.
The more I tried sorting things out,
the more it gets complicated.
Couldn't change it, best leave it unsorted.

Trapped and confused in oneself,
realising good is not rewarded,
becoming a hazard to oneself is

emotionally supported,
thoughts aborted,
mind distorted.
Crying for help, misunderstood,
best leaving it unsorted.

My story has been miserably reported,
painting pictures of a dark soul craving for attention.
My good and bad deeds never got recorded.
My mind and thoughts all distorted,
I see your lies already recorded,
your violence has resorted,
my knowledge is distorted.
Easily influenced by money, power
and respect, unfortunately, your care has departed
I pray you to change before disappointed.
In this dead zone, utterly alone
with no alliance sorted.
Twisted, confused and contorted,
life couldn't be fair; a gem gets aborted,
a murderer is born, evil gets rewarded,
this puzzle is disturbingly distorted,
though my salvations worth more than gold yet can't be
rewarded.
We took things for granted,
now our dreams are haunted,
confronted by the same false emotions, we took for
granted.
You had everything you ever wanted.
The freer it was, the more you took it for granted,
don't be sad cause you've got what you ever wanted.
Don't feel bad or be disappointed,
standing stuffed like a soldier undaunted.
Never cared, never wanted,
why are you so disappointed?

Haunted, taunted, that's what you've
always wanted.
The hunter now becomes the hunted.
And here comes the dark darkness you always wanted.
Temptation took over it and now you're haunted
you set yourself apart, no fingers need be pointed.

In a mile of blue lights, guns are pointed,
toward the enemy within most wanted,
you were always confronted
though you took it for granted.
My bad rhymes were ungracefully plotted,
to suit the haters most wanted,
now secluded, guilty and remorsefully disappointed.

CHAPTER 3 - DISCRIMINATION

Nazek Ramadan

Nazek Ramadan is the founder and executive director of Migrant Voice, a charity that aims to raise the profile and confidence of migrants in the media and public life, ensuring public debate on migration reflects the people it affects.

It is a sad fact that discrimination is as prevalent as ever. Whether intentional or not, discrimination based on race, religion, gender, sexual orientation, age, ethnicity, class or any other feature or status strikes at our most basic human rights. When I read these stories and poems, it evoked memories of the racism I faced when I first arrived in the UK in 1986, having fled my home in Beirut. As a migrant in this country, all I wanted was to be accepted and make a safe home for my family and me. Home is at the heart of every migrant and refugee, the desire to find a safe place and feel safe and at home.

I believe that much of the negative attitude to migrants is based on ignorance, compounded by propaganda conveyed through various media. Those who hold racist attitudes don't know the real human stories of the people they are attacking – these people are simply statistics without faces. When you don't know someone or know their story, it is easy to hate from a distance. It is only through personal accounts such as those in this chapter that migrants can become visible and develop a positive relationship with others. There is capacity for learning for all parties, accepting others even if they are different to us, accepting lifestyles even if different to ours, accepting beliefs even if different to ours. Accepting is not adopting; it is merely welcoming another person as an individual, not a statistic.

The stories in this chapter are the introduction to open and frank dialogue where sharing and understanding can be reached. I urge you to read them and relate to the authors' circumstances and situations.

My Life as an Immigrant, in so Many Words

Farisai Dzemwa

> Farisai Dzemwa, migrated to the United Kingdom
> over ten years ago, after having experienced trauma
> in her native Zimbabwe. Her story reflects the
> discrimination she faced from both colleagues and
> strangers. Despite this, she remains positive and
> confident that she can overcome any barriers and
> be a positive presence in her community.

I stepped out of the revolving doors feeling like a million dollars but all they saw was an overdressed and wrongly dressed immigrant.

"Here comes another one", they must have said to each other as I passed them.

"Another job will be stolen soon", another would probably have said.

"Or maybe, live in luxury on our sweat, step into the benefit system and never come out", "I hate these migrants, ignorant, lazy, parasites and thieves", he continued.

The last statement is the part I heard said out loud and I wondered who they were talking about as I walked past them; for I never imagined it could have been me. To start with, I had never heard the word immigrant before, except reading it in a novel, and at that point it was only a word that helped shape the story that I was reading, fiction that's all.

On the other hand, even if they had added my name in their name-calling, thoughts, and conversations, I still would have thought they were talking about someone else, another Farisai, for my view of myself was way above that. My being here was supposed to have been a short-term diversion, a therapeutic pathway to finding myself again after trauma had struck me back home in Zimbabwe. A situation that seemed to follow me everywhere I went around my country until l was at breaking point.

But months later, reflecting, after I heard another label thrown at me in the workplace, I knew without a shred of doubt that what I had heard those months before was assumptions being made about me and that made me mad.

"Look at her, working non-stop, practically lives here. She thinks she will be promoted to director soon. Making us look bad", one co-worker complained to her colleague in the staff room while we were on our break.

I acknowledge I had been working hard. Long hours and almost every day of the week for weeks on end because that was another therapeutic pathway for my tormented heart, mind, and soul. The effects of the violation I had suffered back home seemed unwilling to loosen its hold on me even this far away. So, I worked myself into stupor everyday so that I would slumber at night in exhaustion and not have to toss and turn in agony of unwanted memories.

Yet again, all they saw was another black immigrant bent on disturbing their peace by stealing from their resources. Isn't it ironic that even as I contributed to the economy, I was still called a thief? Is it not ironic still, that even as I did the hard and exhausting jobs that they avoided anyway, I was still seen as a problem that they would throw out in an instant if they had a chance? "Where is the love?", I thought to myself. The "one world, one people" notion I had been taught growing up.

I blinked back the tears feeling like I was stuck between a rock and a hard place. I could not be back home because it represented a set of problems and yet being here, I saw myself piling on another set of problems, but of a different kind. "Lord, where do the souls of the broken find rest", I remember thinking as I sat there eating my peanut butter sandwich and even today while in reflection.

Though I have managed to turn my life around, achieved a great deal both for myself and for my community, I am still carrying baggage of torment. As I have finally managed to drop the baggage that pushed me out of my own country, I have ironically found myself carrying another, full of the torment that comes with discrimination, racism, exclusion, minimisation, and disrespect. The name calling has continued and the accusations too. Thief, asylum seeker, parasite, ignorance, a hard-to-reach community, loud, aggressive, ugly and HERO.

Isn't it ironic that I say HERO without pleasure? This is because l do not feel like a hero as I find myself working on the frontline, risking my life because l know l have no choice but to work there even after being flagged as a higher risk of contracting the ferocious demonic virus COVID-19. My greatest hope is that the antibodies in my system from contracting the virus at the beginning of the pandemic will keep long enough. Either until the virus is eradicated or until I get the vaccine (another scary thought).

Yet, I smile as I reflect, because life has taught me some lessons and I feel the need to share them; for acknowledgement of lessons learned is citation of one's own growth, development and maturity. The ability to make lemon juice with the lemons that life throws at you. That, I can safely claim to be proud of.

Hidden in the ironies of my life as an immigrant is the lesson that running away from problems is not always the answer because life is, in fact, a combination of problems and achievements. Thus, I am here to stay and continue to make something of myself and of my community, overcoming whatever barriers arising as I go.

After all, I believe home is where the heart is, and my heart is right here in Bilston.

Old Church (Manchester, 1968)

Abida Akram

Abida was born in the Punjab in Pakistan. She came
to England with her mother and sister to join her
father, whom she had never met, in the mid-1960s.
The trauma of leaving her beloved extended family
behind was huge. The bewildering journey, lack of
English, and the first few lonely cold years in England
are forever etched in her memory. And it is these
memories of being a migrant that inspired her writing.
Abida is proud of doing well in a country that does
not always make it easy to belong or to be successful.

Red brick, terraced houses in lines, street after street,
full to the brim with mill working families,
surrounding vast rectangular shadows of cotton mills.

A dark outline, rectangular too,
a steep triangle of a roof.
The old church abandoned at night,
all hard edges of stone, slate, flagstones.
A massive tree in the darkest corner of its yard
conversing, whispering to itself,
a mass of shivering leaves
on a warm night breeze in June.

The whoop, whoop, of laughter disturbs.
Boys shouting,
'Come on Joe, I dare'st you ...'
'This way Trevor'.
'Andr...' – names, quickly cut off by hands slapped over
mouths.
Slap of shoes on flagstones.

Heads bobbing over the brick wall,
arms held high in an arc,
sharp crack as a stone
hits a bedroom window.
The target: the immigrant house.
Rattle, as other stones hit back yards and shed roofs.
Lights come on in upstairs windows.
Immigrants never sleep soundly,
fearful of waking up to more graffiti on their front door,
smashed windows at the back.

Loud laugher, many shushes ...
quick patter and slap of shoes running away.

The immigrant children kept vigil all night,
hardly able to keep their eyes open at school the next
day.

Please Question your Misconceptions

Sisi Wang

> Sisi Wang, originally from China, grew up in Slovakia.
> Her family came to the UK in 2014. As a young writer,
> she wanted to share her story because she feels her
> experience isn't unique and is in fact relatable to many
> young people who left their home countries to come
> to the UK. Moreover, Sisi wants to achieve a sense of
> understanding from others who never have to feel this
> way or don't realise that the feeling of being foreign
> could be so vivid and intricate.

The feeling of being an outsider cannot be understood
until it's felt. You fear that you are only welcome when
you are the version of yourself that they like. The
pressure, the judgement, and the desperation to feel
accepted, is crushing. You implode. You try to fit into
a society that doesn't have space for you unless you
are needed. You can't be understood when they are so
certain that they already understand. Your individuality
is irrelevant when they identify you with stereotypes and
presumptions and generalisations.

　　As an impressionable 11-year-old girl, I
leaned into all my stereotypes because it made me feel
understood, liked, relatable. I wear the taffeta dress, I
agree politely, I smile sweetly as if I'm not currently
suffering from an identity crisis. I contemplate whether
I would be a completely different person if I came to
this country later in my life. Of course, I would. I saw a
society that didn't reflect my culture and my experiences,
but I kept telling myself that I could belong, regardless
of our differences. There's an ocean between my external
self and … me. Will I ever stop feeling like an outsider?

The girl with the ecstatic smile and her library books and her gleaming school shoes and her big group of friends, felt lonely. Setting discrimination, bias, and injustice aside, this girl just wanted to be herself; not representative of or represented by factors that are arbitrary. "What did the colour of my skin, the shape of my eyes or the ethnicity box that I ticked, have anything to do with the unique person that I am," she asked. "Everything," they answered. Always being a minority in the room means that it is demanded of you to have a voice that is representative of a rich, fascinating, and complicated culture. It's scary when your seat at the table is contingent on understanding someone else's culture and experiences. Exclusion because of your differences and 'otherness'. You are invited to a costume party and the theme is to dress like a British person.

I am proud of my cultural background, and I accept that it's a part of me, but tolerance and diversity should look like learning about each other's cultures and embracing it. We should not be colour-blind and tone-deaf to the cultural moment and our innate differences. When the cashier at my favourite local café backed away from the counter and openly said, "I am not taking these customers with Corona," (clearly differentiating me from the previous white customers) my eyes were aggressively pulled open; to fully absorb and understand the dilapidated state of racial discrimination. This is five years after I had arrived in the UK, long after the moment I called this place my home. Some may see nothing wrong with that. Let me paint you this picture.

In all the picture books that I've read growing up, the princess has had blond hair, blue eyes, and fair skin. I couldn't be a princess. I joined a school that played rounders and netball, sports I had never even heard of before. Naturally there's no way I can get on the A team.

I couldn't do it but I learnt, didn't I. Fast forward five years, I've studied the culture, played the sport, learnt the colloquialism, spoken the accent, eaten strawberries at Wimbledon, boarded at school, lost some mates over the years, bought the tuck, worn the uniform, been to Henley and Ascot, drank the tea, taken a cab, watched the Rugby, fancied a boy, driven on the left side of the road, taken the tube, said "sorry" unnecessarily, talked about the weather, queued in queues, asked matron to put me off games, passed CEs, GCSEs and doing A-levels, kept my emotions at bay, appreciated the NHS, folded crisps into a sandwich but how come I still feel so foreign, so 'othered'. So, I wonder if I will ever feel at home, feel included, feel recognised for more than just my labels. Disclaimer, I refer to "they" as some people, not all people.

Is this temporary? Do I grow out of it? I feel very privileged to have made friends and found people of which I align with morally, politically, philanthropically and in terms of ideas regarding social change. We learnt about each other's cultures, experiences, and hardships and although we are completely unique and unable to relate, we created a space for people standing at the intersections of communities, with equally important voices.

Thank you, truly, for taking the time to hear my story.

TGIUK

Immigrants Blues

Michael Ndoun

> This is the final poem in a trilogy that Michael
> has written to showcase the struggle of a troubled
> man who has been destroyed in the pursuit of
> freedom. It reflects the depth of discrimination
> and humiliation faced by those of 'dark skin'.

They say I'm dirty and a drain from a shit hole nation.
This dirty drain is now a pain to a whole nation.
Dark skin circumcised by a predator with a skin colour
notion.
Dark skin, right sin, white skin, right promotion.
The humiliation continues to define the manuscript of
my identity in slow motion
wrapped up in a pathetic portion.
Self-mutilation has now become my daily portion,
understanding my redemption can only be acquired if I
stop seeking liberation.
What a sad light unfading to a migrant constant
confession.

The shadows of my sorrow yearn for a better tomorrow
with less commotion.
My melanin dictates whether I'm an immigrant or an
expatriate in a land with more human
right motion.
This couldn't be corruption but a correction to a defect
that could falsify a White skin nation.
They say I'm supposed to have thick skin,
I'm supposed to lay down and die because of my skin
colour, repulsion,
so, I started shedding off the layer of my skin,

keeping one step ahead of the prosecutor,
Sin.

This is no imagination or predestination,
my skill is now defined by the uncoloured skin nation.
We'll rise to fight this discrimination,
corruption,
our ancestors paid the price with a change to keep for
my dark skin election.
So marginalised just to see your civilisations.
You say my skin tone is not aesthetics enough,
so, requires no recommendation.
Your civil right is bad with no contrition.

Machiavelli was your plan to dethrone the civilisation of
a Black nation,
to kill a dog, you had to accuse him
of having rabies from a dark skin nation.
This is from a nation with a human heart,
that changes like a chameleon with no consideration.
With a human mind that is full of
extreme intellect of terror and delusion,
with a human mouth that has the tongue of torture with
brutal incisions.

This dark skin species couldn't be the
smartest of all.
Delineated as domestic animals,
bred in cages to feed, to work, to please,
to comfort and to ease the pain of a
stainless nation.
Dark skin with no nation,
her master, Prejudice, couldn't be hidden,
her arrogance for her skin colour,
couldn't be missing.

Couldn't be tamed, now left to the range, and roam the
planet
in search of a confiscated destiny.
This is mutiny,
how can I be blamed by the blamed for the blame they
enflamed?
How can I be shamed by the shamed for the game they
framed?
Ironically, I'm free as a bird riding
on the back of wind-assisted shame,
floating down the stream of blame
to proclaim my liberty in shame.

Your dark is evil, and your evil is black.
My pigment makes a White nation
clinch to her purse with straight allegations.
Take the blinders from your vision,
so, you can see the power of segregation.
Take the padding from your ears,
so, you hear the crying of a tearing nation.
Your equality and I will be free with no questions,
your equality, and I will be seen with no impression.

Dark skin with no passion,
they used their finest duplicity
to mock our nudeness with no inclination.
We've laughed to shield out crying tears
whilst shuffling through our dreams,
with great suspicion.
Accustomed to courage,
was the only way to steer our ship to the
right direction.

With blood, sweat, and tears

we paid the price, though it wasn't fair.
Stolen from the cradle of our comfort,
Smears,
weeping for being stripped of our culture,
steers.

Your fantasies are captivated by a wicked soul,
infatuated with the dark skin melanin.
You fought hard to distort the achievements
we erected,
and now our crowning achievement is to dismantle the
great tombs you erected.

CHAPTER 4 - MAKING A LIFE

Jonathan Portes

Jonathan Portes is a Professor of Economics and
Public Policy at King's College London, a senior
fellow at the UK in Changing Europe, and author
of *What Do We Know And What Should We Know
About Immigration* (2019).

I began working on the economics of immigration and
integration as a civil servant over 25 years ago. I'm an
economist, most at home with data and statistics, and I
firmly believe that the evidence shows that immigrants
make the UK a better place, whether economically,
socially, or culturally. However, behind the numbers are
real people. Immigrants and refugees are human beings;
each has a story to tell. From Alf Dubs, who arrived
on the Kindertransport in 1939, to the frightened
Afghan boy stepping off a dinghy on the Kent coast in
November 2021, the majority of people, migrants and
refugees, who come to our country are searching for a
better life, a safer life and a happier life.

This chapter has some of their stories. You
will learn of a young girl who, despite having limited
English when she first arrived, is now studying Maths
at university, and of another young woman wanting to
learn English so she can speak up at work. They are
not just "economic migrants", and they are certainly not
here to take advantage of our welfare state; they are part
of our future. And their challenges are our challenges:
what could be more British than a young boy finding
his friendship group through playing football or a young
woman enduring the hardships of the rental market in
London?

Most people who look at the evidence understand that immigration benefits the British economy, from the NHS and care homes to universities and restaurants. But nevertheless, it remains a deeply contentious political and social issue. In part, that reflects a lack of understanding of what immigration and immigrants can give us not just as workers but as people. I hope this book goes some way to changing that.

Girl like Me

Sonja Morgenstern

As one of the prize winners in the TGIUK
Storytelling competition, Sonja tells of how she first
visited London in the summer of 1995. She moved
to live in London in 1996 to make a life with her then
boyfriend, a young man she met in that first summer.
She tells of how she made a life and a family in the
UK but left in 2019 following Brexit, to return to her
home country.

"There's not much room to dance".
I had to ask the tall, skinny blonde lad next to me to
repeat himself three times; the pumping reggae music
was drowning out his voice, and I was unfamiliar with his
cockney accent. "Yes, right …" I replied, or something
like that. He caught on that I was foreign, and I told him
I was from Germany, on holiday in England for the first
time and had read about the Notting Hill Carnival in a
guidebook. It was 1995.

We bopped along to the music, watching the
floats and costumes; we were both 18 years old. He told
me about his 11 siblings, and I explained I'd been to an
acting workshop, spent a few days enjoying Viking Bay
in Broadstairs, and was now on my final week of the
summer holidays in London. He gave me his number
and asked if I would go out with him one evening. I
felt a flush of excitement, having never been asked out
before, and carefully pocketed the slip of paper.

The next day, I somehow lost the piece of paper
with the lad's work number on at the British museum
and spent the rest of the afternoon thumbing the phone
book and calling directory enquiries with my pocket

change, to track down my new crush. It was in vain. Somehow, I'd underestimated how hard it would be to track down a skinny 18-year-old that lived with a flatmate in Ilford, having just a surname to go on, in a city of close to 10 million people.

Eventually, defeated, I stepped out into the street to get some dinner on my own. To my surprise, the lad was walking towards me almost as soon as I left the youth hostel! He told me that when he hadn't heard from me, he had made his way over straight from work to find me. He wined and dined me at some diner in Leicester Square, and I felt like a princess in a fairy tale.

That evening, he walked me home along the banks of the Thames, singing "I've never met a girl like you before", and we kissed for the first time in the street outside the YHA. His kissing, much like the quality of his suit, was awful but I tried not to mind as I was falling in love with him.

I went back to Germany, and we kept in touch by letter and phone calls, the latter playing a role in his abrupt night-time move out from his flat share, and back in with his large family. When a phone bill for the flat came, he decided to leg it, as it was over £200, more than a week's wages.

When my autumn half-term holiday came around, I flew back to visit him, lucky to have a bed of my own in his sisters' bedroom, who topped and tailed in bunkbeds. The dad used to be a boxer and had left most of his teeth in the boxing ring; he chain smoked with the baby on his lap while the older kids performed Irish dancing in the living room. The mum brought me proper cups of English tea with two sugars.

In December, I was back again. This time, the lad told me he'd invested in a 'very nice hotel' near Finsbury Park, which turned out to be a cheap B&B

with holes in the windows which I stuffed with my socks to avoid freezing. The breakfast sausages came sliced in half lengthways, and I met a nice gay couple who were staying there to escape the Brixton riots.

New Year's Eve was disappointing. There were no fireworks, and by the stroke of midnight we were still rushing down Brick Lane to a warehouse party near Eli's Yard, where the lad worked. Eli was his boss, and Eli's Yard was still a working clothes import business then.

A year after meeting the lad, September 1996, I moved to London. By then the lad had bought his own flat; unbelievably grown-up to a school leaver from Germany, who hadn't even decided what to do with her life yet!

But first, London. I happily played housewife aged 19, and we shared his ex-council flat near the Blackwall Tunnel with a view of Canary Wharf. I had landed an internship with a TV production company, where I was paid the cost of my weekly travel card. The lad's wage packet came in cash, wrapped in brown paper on a Friday, and he'd go to the bank on Saturday, his only day off, to pay the mortgage.

When my internship ended, I got a job in a clothes store on Oxford Street, where I quickly learned to sell the right pair of jeans to suit any body shape. I was paid £3.65 per hour and worked part-time so I was able to spend the lad's day off with him every week. We visited my family in Germany at Christmas, and because work didn't want to give me the time off, I quit.

When I got back to the London flat a day after the lad, it was freezing. Thinking this would save money, he'd decided to turn off the gas and I couldn't get the heating on. So, I ran a bath, which sat steaming in the tub, tempting me to get in. I stripped off and put my foot in, expecting to quickly warm up in some bubbles, but I discovered the water was icy cold. I hadn't yet worked out the connection between the hot water in the radiators, and the water used to run a bath ... so, I waited for him in bed, under all the covers we had and my winter coat. It was New Year's Eve 1996. The lad and I split up a few months later, and I began living with friends who I'd met through my new job.

I stayed living in London until 2019. By then I had acquired a British home, degree, career, and child, but Brexit forced me to reconsider my future in Britain, nonetheless.

I am a British citizen by naturalisation but couldn't see an immediate future in a country which was so divided and seemed so hostile suddenly. When a workmate of the lad's asked him, in 1997, "How is your Nazi bitch?", the lad gave him a black eye.

In 2016, the hostility was more subtle, but no less toxic. The newspaper headlines on June 24th shocked me to the core. Was this where I wanted my son to grow up? I struggle with fitting in in Germany, it is much harder adjusting 'back home' than it ever was adjusting to life in the UK.

Changes

Erin Bresler

Erin was born in South Africa and moved to the United Kingdom when she was nine years of age. This is her prize winning story and reflects the challenges and new experiences facing migrants, through the eyes of a child.

You are nine years old. Your life is normal, well at least you believe it to be. Your biggest problems are where you want to put your favourite teddy bear and which Barbie movie to watch after supper. You don't know how much your life can change in such a short time.

Terminal 3. As you step out of the airplane, an icy wind engulfs you. The sky is enclosed by soft charcoal clouds. You take a deep breath in, and the bitterly cold air hits the back of your throat. The wind swerves between the leaves on oak trees that are placed in an orderly line. The condensation on the windows along the walkway have crystallised into minuscule patterns. You analyse every crystal structure as you meander along the hallway, your purple hand luggage drags along behind you. Each crystal is unique, not one crystal is like the last. It fascinates you, although they may be similar, there are still minute details that make them different. The stark contrast between this wintery environment and the hot, sunny, dry place you have always called home is overwhelming.

As you wait for your London taxi-cab with all your worldly possessions stacked up in six suitcases, your mind again flicks back to all that you've left behind. Family, friends, school, pets and so many memories. Why did your parents make this drastic decision? The enormity of what has just happened and where you are now hits you.

You are used to hot, dry weather. Christmas is in summer as opposed to winter, so when the Christmas music was about winter wonderlands, you never experienced what that was like.

What you thought was normal is surprising to other people. You have to live in an estate, otherwise it's too dangerous. If you didn't live in an estate, you would have six and a half foot high walls with electric fencing surrounding your house. Police with AK47s instead of regular pistols roam around the shopping malls. They wave them about as if they are a toy. Your bag has to be shoved under your seat when in a car to avoid people smashing your window. The best way you would describe most of the people is careless and dangerous. Ramping pavements and running red lights, the roads are manic. But it's your home. It's where you learned to ride a bike, had your first crush, took your first steps, said your first words. It's home. It's where you grew up for nine years. Although you have moved, it will always be your home. The mountains worth of memories you've made there will never fade away.

As you gaze out of the pine needle scented taxi-cab, you realise that the roads are quiet except from the engine noise. No honking, no banging of metal, just subtle engine noise. Nothing like what you're used to. There are no street vendors knocking on your window and trying to convince you to buy an illegal copy of a DVD. It surprises you, but you're also relieved.

The lights of London illuminate your face. People wander along the city streets, window shopping in the expensive stores. It seems safe, no one is looking over their shoulder to see if anyone is following them. This confuses you but also makes you feel comfortable.

Your life has been full of precautions to ensure that you stayed safe. This was never weird to you because it was something you did naturally, you did every time you got in the car. You had an escape plan if anyone was ever to break into the car, if someone grabbed you, you would need to scream. You never realised that this wasn't normal.

You don't know what to expect when it comes to school. Things are so different. As time has passed, you have felt anxious about making new friends. As you walk into the school reception you feel the gaze of your soon to be classmates. You are the new kid, the one that everyone will talk about, the one that everyone wants to know about but is too scared to talk to. A tall smiley woman strides out of the office. She seems to be the headteacher, she starts to talk to your parents. You don't pay attention; you are too interested in the classrooms that you can peer into from where you're standing. There are words in a different language written across the walls. A large "Bonjour" is slapped on the front of the door. You assume it's French. The woman calls over an assistant.

"Can you grab Katherine for me please, she's in 4G". She continues to talk to your parents; she's talking about some relatives who lives in the same neighbourhood as we used to.

A small girl rushes through. Her hair is just as long as yours. Her eyes seem to twinkle as she looks you up and down. Her presence lights up the room. She's a teacher's pet. The headteacher turns around and a wide grin appears on her face.

"This is Erin, she is joining the school today and you are going to be her buddy", she says gesturing to you.

"Erin, this is Katherine. She will show you

everything you need to see."

A friend. Well maybe we will be friends. A sense of reassurance; she can introduce you to more people and maybe this won't be as bad as you assumed. You have always been friendly and never been afraid to put yourself out there but after moving country and school, that sense of confidence is less than it previously was.

As you wave your parents goodbye, Katherine energetically grabs your bag and rushes down the hallway.

"Hi! I'm Katherine but you already know that it's nice to meet you!"
Her excitement confuses you. Why is she so comfortable around a person she's never met before?

"It's nice to meet you too," you say cautiously, knowing your accent will draw attention to yourself. As you walk through the school, you realise that the classes are very small, the whole school is very small. Your old school goes from grade triple nought to matric (Year 12 in the UK). The oldest people you can see can't be over the age of eleven. You are confused as to why the school is so small. There is no assembly hall, there is no outdoor swimming pool and there is only one small field.

"Your accent is weird, where are you from?" she asks you with a puzzled expression. You look back at her with mixed emotions.

"I'm from South Africa".

Just a Little Girl in a Completely Different World

Natalia Tamargo Pumisacho

Natalia was born in Spain, to a Spanish father and an Ecuadorian mother. She came to the UK when she was five years of age and has lived in London for the past 12 years. She was motivated to share her prize-winning story as she had a tough time when she first arrived, witnessing family and friends go through the same difficult experiences. She is keen to let migrants, especially her Latin-American community, know that nothing in life comes easy but if you work hard and try your best it will be worth it in the end.

New beginnings can be really challenging in some circumstances, especially for a 5-year-old. Arriving in a whole new world can be really exciting, then facing reality was one of the hardest things I had to do at a very young age.

It was waking up to an alarm clock and mum not being next to me as she had already left for work. Going into school, looking around and not being able to make friends; the language barrier was something hard to face as it made me feel like I was a strange creature to them. I would go home every afternoon to lie in bed, cry and just beg mum to go back to Spain. It was just her and me, so I guess it made this big step so much harder as I missed my dad and other family members that had stayed in Spain.

After some time, a girl approached me, I remember sitting down at a bench and the girl just said in Spanish 'Are you alright?' That day I felt so happy because I used to be very talkative, but I was only able to communicate in Spanish, so it was hard until the girl came up to me and she really did cause some sort of relief in me as I knew I wasn't the only one who spoke Spanish. From that day she helped me so much and taught me how to speak English. Sadly, just as I was getting comfortable at this school, we had to move out of the place we were staying, and this meant changing school.

At that time, I thought changing schools would be nice and nothing new, but I struggled as I began my new primary school. I knew a little English, so it was a bit easier, but I still struggled to make friends and feel comfortable in this new environment.

A few months went past, and I had made friends, I had finally settled in quite well and was able to be very comfortable with the language. I had made friends that spoke Spanish but after a while without noticing I had friends that spoke English and I was able to communicate very good with them. I was also helping kids that were new to the school and they only spoke Spanish to settle in; it was something I loved doing as I had gone through that horrible time where I felt so different to others, and I didn't want anyone to feel like that.

I wasn't only helping kids but family members and close friends, translating paperwork, following them places to help them out and even teaching them some English so that it would be a bit easier for them to communicate.

Going into secondary was much easier as I was so much more confident, I had no problem with starting at a new place apart from making friends, which I made very quick. I was also told that there was a teacher who supported EAL students and when I met her, I knew she

EAL - English as an Additional Language

was someone very special. She's so dedicated to helping kids that don't know English learn the language, support them throughout their secondary school journey and even after, when they aren't there anymore, as she has done for me.

Lately I have been receiving a lot of recognition for what I used to do and to this day, even if it's something very small, I'll try help anyone. This experience has made me realise that if you keep pushing, you will reach all your goals. I will always fight for my Latin-American community and I would like my story to be a message to foreign people struggling with settling in a society by letting them know they are not alone, that they are capable to learn English and even if it takes months or even years it doesn't matter, cause at the end of the day we will all be able to say "WE'VE DONE IT".

TGIUK

Work with me on my Accent

Alicja Pyszka-Franceschini

Alicja came to the UK after Poland became an official member state of the European Union in 2004. Her aim was to become as competent as possible in English and to mesmerise people with her British accent when she returned to Poland. Her plans changed when she met her husband. She has stayed in the UK to raise her two multilingual children and has been developing her interests in writing, psychology, and visual arts.

With a desperate plea of humid eyes,
with a body that could hold no more,
'Help me with my speech'
– she said to me.
'I just giggle,
I cannot speak
in my meetings.
My throat feels sore
I must stop false believing.
I must let it go.'

And so, we practised,
long and short vowels,
fox and forks,
done and dawn,
ship and sheep,
mill and meal,
hill and heel.
give and receive.

And we found pleasure in repeating the sounds,
and making our lips and faces go in new directions.

There was a joy there,
discovery of sorts;
the sounds cannot be managed
with texts just read alone.

And it surprised me
that I was needed there.
That a teacher was required
to bring out what was there,
the beauty,
the smile,
the voice,
so calmly found,
as if it was my task
to make it hers
but no longer home-bound.
To stop her saboteur.
To let her tongue become
a serene interpreter.
Because she had gifts to share
and no more time to spare.

And then we talked,
and we were honest,
that no amount of practice
will make us feel at ease,
for English was at times
almost like Japanese.
So different,
and so odd.
Don't mind me saying so.

Exotic is beautiful.
Exotic is good.
But I am blushing at my meetings,
because I don't know the rules.

I know,
I know ,
time to transfer.
Time to concur.
We're leaving fears behind,
without the time to spare.

Let's just do the work.
Let's be creative.
Accent is not an obstacle
to remain emancipated.

It's the work that counts.
Speech will follow its commands.

TGIUK

A Bowl of Soup

Natalie Gregory

Natalie's country of origin isn't quite so straight forward. Her father is German, and her mother was Thai, but she was born in the Philippines, where her family stayed until she was 10 years of age. They moved to Indonesia and finally to Bangkok, where she graduated from a British International School, which inspired her – in 2003 – to travel to the UK for the first time to study English and History at the University of York. Natalie fell in love with an English boy. Marriage, and two kids later and she is still here. Her story was one of the prize winners.

The day Dao discovers that Ma is a witch is so cold that the children dare each other to lick the school fence, their tongues briefly sticking to the frozen metal bars.

'The witch is coming,'
Dao hears them whisper. Most run and hide. The bolder ones crowd around to gawk. Ma's skin glows as if the sun is shining through the clouds, and her black hair floats open around her waist. She just appears out of the fog so, that day, even the bigger kids run. All except for Kev McKinley.

Kev, who started the witch thing, has licked the frostiest metal bar and now Kev is stuck. He pushes against the fence, fat bottom wriggling, but he can't break free. As Ma reaches the gate, Kev squeals. She lifts her hand. Dao holds her breath. Maybe she will turn him into a pig. But Ma just waves and smiles. Then Kev's mother is there to unstick and scold him. She jumps a little when she notices Ma, then drags her son away.

Dao pulls Ma away too, so fewer people can see

that Ma's hilltribe jacket is threadbare. So fewer people can hear Ma's bangles jangle around her wrist. They turn into the street where the cold house huddles against other identical brick houses.

'Come in quickly.' Ma says, opening the door, 'and take off your coat. We're home now.'
Dao shakes her head. She still feels cold. Ma shrugs.

'Nice to be home, na?'

She says the word home a lot when they are inside the red house, repeats it like a spell. Dao begins to doubt the other kids. Then she thinks of Kev's frightened bottom and smiles. Dao hangs up her bag and notices her sister's empty peg.

Where is Pear?' she asks.

'At Anna's,' Ma says.
Pear has friends. And when they came here, Pear already knew things; like what a coat peg and what Dairy Milk was. Dao doesn't know anything.

'I'm hungry,' Dao says.

'Let's get a snack.'

Ma leads the way into the kitchen, the only warm room in the house. Dao sits at the table, while Ma climbs a step to reach a high cupboard. Dao looks her mother up and down: black hair, milk-tea skin, bright clothes. She is just Ma. But maybe, in this place of white fog and grey rain, she does look different.

'Ma, what's a chink?' Dao asks.
Ma turns around, frowning.

'It's a bad word for someone from China.'

'But we're not Chinese, are we?'

'No, Dao. We came from Thailand.'

'So why do they think you're a chink?'

'Sometimes people just don't know better.'
Dao does not tell Ma that they also call her a witch. She does not want to hurt her feelings. Ma finds the biscuits

and hands one to her.

'Ma.'

'Yes, Noo.'

'I want to go home.'

'This is home, Noo. This is our home now.'

Ma says it twice again, like a broken spell. Dao bites her lip, but Ma can see the tears before they fall. She rushes over to hug her.

'Noo, shall we have something special for dinner?' Ma asks.

Dao nods. Ma heats up silky-white coconut cream. She adds leaves and stalks, roots and bulbs to the pot. Familiar smells fill the room: sweet with lemongrass, hungry with garlic.

Ma fetches a straw mat and spreads it on the linoleum floor next to the big radiator. Dao sits cross-legged on the mat, as close to the radiator as she dares. From here the tiny kitchen looks bigger and instead of the backs of other houses, the window now frames the distant beckoning sky. In her wool coat, Dao starts to thaw happily. Then she notices Ma's precious photo hanging above the sink. A black and white younger Ma, draped in a long cape is reaching forward, head bowed before the King.

'Why were you wearing that funny dress?' Dao asks.

'Because I was graduating.'

'What's that?'

'It's when you finish studying and get a diploma.'

'That magic scroll the King is giving you?'

'Yes.' Ma laughs, 'It gives you the power to get a good job.'

Jobs are the reason they have come to this country. It is why Dad goes out every day to a special place to find work.

'So why don't you have a job, Ma?' Dao asks.

'When would I have time?'

Ma is very busy; cooking, cleaning, sewing. She fixes things in the house. Like when that rock smashed through the front window. Ma patched it with cardboard until the council put in new glass.

'When I graduate,' Dao says, 'will the King give me a scroll?'

Ma cocks her head.

'Only at Thammasat University.'

'Where's that?' Dao asks.

'In Bangkok, but you need to speak Thai to study there, Noo.'

Dao thinks of all those painful afternoons when her and Pear had to sit and copy the sing-song voice on the cassette. Ma was annoyed because Dao got the tones wrong again. Then there was reading and writing, tracing symbols that had heads and tails. They looked like animals or people. They told a story, just not the one Ma wanted her to read. But at least they had been home, where it was warm, where her friends were.

'If I promise to learn Thai, Ma,' Dao says, 'can we go back home, please?'

Ma does not answer. She goes to stir the soup, tapping the spoon on the edge of the pot like a wand.

'It's ready,' she croons.

They eat their tom kha gai sitting on the mat in the warmth of the radiator. Dao feels cocooned in the coconutty broth. When she slurps the last drops straight from the bowl, a little bit dribbles down her chin. Dao wipes it up with her palm and licks that too. Ma is a witch, and her potions work better than her spells; she can fly across oceans with you, all in a bowl of soup.

Nine Lives

Mariana Serapicos

Mariana Serapicos was born in Brazil to a Portuguese father and a Brazilian mother. She moved to the UK in 2012 to pursue a Masters in Filmmaking. Then, she was introduced to the nomadic London lifestyle and after living in nine different houses in nine years, she had to create her own concept of "home". Her winning entry will connect with many readers.

This year, I entered both my ninth year in the UK and my ninth house. I'm living an imposed nomadic life; an experience I share with many people my generation. Forget the property ladder, all we want is a room of one's own.

I grew too big, I think; my life expanded in ways I hadn't planned for. I hate that, I hate that the fact women are meant to feel small, to become small, and to have small possessions by default. Our personalities are meant to fit a size 6, our voices are meant to live inside our heads. We are our own worst enemies, that's what society would like us to think. No. Think big.

I arrived in this country with two suitcases and a rucksack. I remember almost being sent to Dublin at Heathrow Airport when my fresh-from-the-airplane accent could hardly pronounce the tube stop I had to head for. The tube doesn't take you to many places in São Paulo, my hometown, and I was marvelled to see how the landscape changed all the way to Zone 6.

1 My new house had stairs, stairs! I had lived in flats all my life; São Paulo is built upwards – it's like Brazilians are trying to reach the sky. My previous life had been flat, no steps; in London, my room was on the second floor. My arms ached when I reached the small square, I was to call room. I had a single bed, I was used to that, that's how it had been back home, living with my mum.

2   I moved again in December, and my cab fought the snow on a Friday night, charging me extra for the ride. I almost froze to death on the first night, I didn't have any bedding – I shivered under the sheets. It was a three-bed flat without a living room; I used to dry my clothes on the radiators and my mum was worried about the humidity. I had a double bed and two housemates who became friends.

3   I finally left the sticks and moved to Zone 3, to live in a house with no friends and a mouse. My room had a lock, the landlord was always about, my housemates changed on a weekly basis. I had dinner with my mum most nights, chatting to her over Skype. I moved out in the speed of light; I arranged my few belongings in a couple of boxes and 'ran' for dear life.

4   My new house could pass for a hostel, friends, boyfriends, girlfriends lived there, Australians, Argentinians, teachers, and actors. We'd shoot films in the bathroom, danced with the lamp, and did yoga anywhere. The shower leaked in the kitchen, we didn't dare go to the basement, we had a trampoline in the back garden. It was a weird time; it was a fun time. But our lease was up and the musical chairs that is the renting market in London started again.

5   "The dream house" was the next one; we weren't the most obvious fit, but somehow, we felt the four of us would work. We had parties, I had too much absinthe, we'd go in each other's rooms and talked about music and films. This place had no leaks, no mice, no funny noises, the house was functional – it was a shame that we weren't. Eventually the cracks that we could barely see in the beginning of the year became obvious to everyone. That group, in the shape that it was, couldn't go on; we had to re-arrange our formation.

6   I moved south of the river for the first time; I downgraded to a single bed, timing was bad, I finally had a boyfriend to share a bed with. My stuff was everywhere, it didn't fit in the bedroom. 'You are taking up space,' said my housemate - I had a chair. "Coming over here" and placing my belongings on freshly clean carpets, that was me.

7   London favours monogamy; it's much cheaper to share a room with someone. I too jumped on that boat. It came naturally to me, living with a boy, with my partner, my other half – whatever people call it. We had our space, I didn't have to ask for permission, I didn't have to check, we could just talk amongst ourselves. I didn't have to be 'on' all the time, I could just be.

8   Then my partner bought a house, and I thought 'that's it, no more moving around.' I could feel my shoulders drop, I would never have to put my things in a box, book a van or get bubble wrap. I could put nails on the wall, I would actually be able to decorate, put my prints on frames. It was ours; it was home. But regardless of the work that was put into it, it didn't work – not the house, but us. As the world fell apart, so did we, and I had to choose what things to keep. This continuous process involves forced spring cleaning, trips to the charity shop, selling things online, binning old birthday cards.

9   As I noticed myself having to shrink, to make things fit, I realised how I can carry the biggest things within. I can inflate all my possessions in an invisible way; they don't take actual space. The family, the friends that I made, the memories, the drunk nights and park walks, dancing in the kitchen, because, why not? All this lives within me. They have carried me all this time, and I them.

They are just a screen away, and elbow shake. Through all those moves, they were there, in all my homes – because that's what they are. All those rooms morphed into something meaningful because life is what you carry inside. The memories, the friends, the books I read; I carry them in my heart.

In Britain

Inna Martinova

Inna came to the United Kingdom from Ukraine on Christmas Day 2019. She wrote this poem to share her experience as a young teenager migrating to a new country and a new society and the cost of severing all ties with her previous life. Her poem reflects her struggle to make friends and how she sometimes feels she is alone in an ocean without the support of family and friends.

Destroying all my plans,
my dad sent me a letter.
He said: "pack all your bags,
I bought you a ticket for Christmas."

The road was long,
but the path that lay ahead
much longer.
And I stepped on it fearlessly.

The English I learned
at school, in my country,
was not the one that I caught
in the conversations of the people around.

New experience, so beautiful!
People, streets, roads, and houses.
Everything is alien, I can't stand it.
For others, only I am a stranger.

I've met people everywhere –
on a walk, in a store, at school.

I found wonderful friends,
But unfortunately, not friends to the grave.

I thought we were going to cross the barrier
succumbing to a wonderful moment,
but a day passed and a new one came.
Over time, I became a shadow.

From time to time, wonderful landscapes helped me;
beautiful cathedrals and fields around.
I never could have thought
that in my heart is the Ukrainian land.

Carrying my longing through the years
I will walk for many more years.
I'll seal my doubts in verse
and with a smile on my face, I will learn this world.

Vulnerabilities

Alicja Pyszka-Franceschini

This is Alicja's second entry and reflects the challenges that migrants face as they begin to adapt to their new home and find their place in a new community. Often to embrace the new, we have to put aside the old, and forget our past. Loneliness plays a key role in those early days and as strangers, we are grateful when a stranger strikes up a simple conversation.

She woke me up with her gratitude for conversation:
'Thank you for talking to me,'
she said to me.
As if a conversation was a gift
that to migrants is never given for free.

I knew how trapped she felt
in words that wouldn't go,
how lonely and how hurt,
because they wouldn't flow.

'Your past doesn't count
when you are here.
What you worked on before
has little or no memory,
and it is difficult to start again
to start from scratch. And be for new people
without a breath to catch.'

Being in a new country
among the people that she didn't know,
a simple chat felt like a gift
that one just couldn't throw.

I knew she needed time,
I knew she needed patience,
to rise above her fears,
she needed questions and my ears.

She had to escape her place of safety,
brave the wildness,
forget about the loved ones that she left behind,
forget about the life that she built elsewhere,
as if the hands that she used to have,
had also to stay there.

'Am I allowed to work here
on things that really count?
Am I allowed to be myself?
And make the world unbound?
Can I fight for justice?
Can I speak my mind?

I haven't done this for a while.
I've been feeling like a fly,
that stays on the wall
and just sits there,
and does nothing.
Can I be myself?
And bring the world my grafik?*'

I want to share myself.
Talk through the joys and through the pain.
Wouldn't it be lovely for all of us to start
talking in a manner
that brings us together
rather than sets us apart?

'Thank you for talking to me',

she said to me.
I saw a friend in her.

Infinite luxury.

* Polish for "schedule"

TGIUK

A Czeched-In Ticket to the UK

Karolina Jaks

Karolina has lived in the UK for over eight years. She moved here with her mother and brother as her mother wanted to give her children the opportunity of a UK education. This is Karolina's story of her journey and her success at her studies.

I was born in the Czech Republic, where I lived for about ten years before we moved to England, and my whole life went downhill. Kind of in a good way, like a perfect drop on a rollercoaster, although I wasn't very happy about it as all I was focusing on was the sheer panic of such a big change.

In the summer of 2013, my brother and I went on a summer camp. It lasted two weeks, and every morning we were taught English, and the rest of the day, we had a new group activity that added up to a camp competition. I vividly remember sitting in our car on the way back home. I was still very excited about the events of the last few days. Our team ended up winning the competition, and I happened to be the one to complete the last task we needed to secure our victory. On top of that, I got excellent feedback from the English teachers.

Looking back, I remember that my English was relatively decent compared to the average 10-year-old in the Czech Republic, but the idea of moving to England was something that wouldn't even cross my mind. I mean, I could barely have a conversation, let alone have all my lessons or ask for assistance in a shop all in English. As I sat there in the car, my smile slowly turned to tears as my mum explained all the upsides to moving away from our family, our school, my friends and generally what I considered a very successful social life when I was 10. I think the thing that stopped me from completely going out of my mind was my mum's reassurance that it'll be just for one year and then we'll go back (except that wasn't true, but more on that later).

So, a few months later, we packed some of our belongings, and on the 8th of October 2013, we flew to the UK. I'm pretty sure we flew to London Luton airport – not that that's relevant in any way. At that time, my aunt had lived in Oxford for a few years so, that was our destination. We lived with her for a bit before moving in with a family that rented us two rooms.

Within about a month, we were all settled into our new home; and despite being utterly terrified, I was going to school for the first time. My mum walked me to school, and we talked to the headteacher. Even though I introduced myself with the Czech pronunciation of my name, the way everybody said my name my whole life, she asked how to pronounce it and only gave two options for the answer; the British versions of the name. That was quite daunting. My life just turned upside down, and now my name is changing too? But I just figured it's better than everybody struggling with saying my name. When I first entered the classroom, the first question was what my name was. I automatically said my name – my actual name – I was really anxious and wasn't really thinking; however, nobody really seemed to have an issue with it, so I thought, "Well, that's convenient!" and moved on. Later, we had an assembly, and the headteacher was making announcements, one of which was that there were two new students in school, me and a younger boy. When she pronounced my name wrong, a lot of the people from my class shouted my actual name in correction, so, since then, that's the name I use, and nobody seems to have too much trouble with it.

When lessons started, I had absolutely no clue what was going on. Now, when I have trouble with schoolwork, I like to use the phrase "might as well be in a foreign language." I love saying that because there was a time when all my schoolwork actually was in a foreign language, and I still remember how challenging and perplexing, that was. I also like saying "might as well be written in Greek" when referring to maths or chemistry as both of those subjects often use letters of the Greek alphabet such as Pi or Delta. The first week I carried around a piece of paper with "I don't understand" written phonetically on it because that was still a bit too advanced for me, and I kept forgetting how to say it. The only subject I slightly understood was maths; 6x3 equals 18 in any language. Plus, I was good at it. The maths level we were at in the Czech Republic was higher than here, so it was just a refresher of the basics but, even when we started learning new stuff, I still enjoyed it, so I put effort into it.

Now we have been in the UK for about seven and a half years, which is considerably longer than one year but I'm happy. Well, I'm a depressed A-level student having to deal with the mess of COVID so, I'm not happy in general; what I mean is I'm happy with the decision to move to England even though I didn't seem to have much say in it. I now prefer English to Czech, and my primary school love of maths, fuelled by its international aspect, turned into a passion. I have a conditional offer to study maths at Warwick University. If everything goes well, I would like to get a PhD in mathematics and work in research, so I got pretty excited well, it's exciting to me, job aspirations out of the move. Not to mention all the amazing friends that I have here in England, without whom I probably wouldn't have made it through seven years away from my family or through a fairly difficult time in my life when I got depression.

TGIUK

New Home

Loraine Masiya Mponela

This is Loraine's third poem in the collection. Here she shares the wonder of being made welcome in a new home. Her poems showcase that migrants live the same life, go to the same schools, and take the same exams as every other person. This is why she appreciates even more the simple act of a smile.

I have been exposed
to the love of strangers.
Seen smiles directed at me
and the smiling eyes
with mouths covered with masks.

It has been eye-opening
to know that so much love exists
in this city.

That a homeless girl can share
a life and be provided with a home
away from home.

It has been a learning curve
to have my privileges checked
closely.

That a Malawian girl can speak
English, possess colourful GCSEs
and an award.

It has been mind-blowing

to experience greatness
alongside great leaders.

I have seen the better side of humanity
love instead of hate.

It warms my heart
that humanity is in a better place
in its care for other humans.

How One Woman Changed my Life

Anthony

Anthony's story reflects the challenges that many second-generation migrant children face as they try to transcend the culture their parents hold dear and the culture of their own country. When adult migrants struggle to connect to their new community, it can impact upon their children. Anthony tells how a kind stranger helped him make that move.

My name is Anthony and I'm 14 years old and live in the United Kingdom. My parents migrated here in about 2003. They told me that at first living here was difficult for them; they had to adjust to a different way of living compared to their life in Africa. One special day, a friend of a friend met my mother, and her name was Prue. I don't remember the events that occurred to my mum meeting her, but I do know that day changed me forever.

When I was about five years old, I wasn't very athletic and couldn't even catch or throw a ball. It meant that I could not play the same games as the other kids on the street. So, Prue suggested that I do a week's sports course to enhance my basic sports skills. I reluctantly agreed, I mean who wants to go to another school after school and ignored the fact that she generously paid for it.

The course was amazing. I remember going through a transformation, my sports skills improved so much, and I became more confident playing ball. I think I didn't thank her then, but I know it was probably the best course I have ever done in my life.

But then there was obviously a problem, I had these skills, but I had nothing to do with them. One day I saw some bigger boys playing football and I was intrigued because I wanted to play with them as well. I asked Prue if I could join in. She gave me the confidence to ask them if I could play and the freedom to be brave. Five minutes later I found myself playing with these massive boys. That is the day my 'football career' started and over the next five years every single Saturday I went to football training. Playing sports made me part of a team, gave me friends with similar interests, gave me a routine, taught me how to commit to my team and helped me develop a sense of loyalty – as well as keeping fit! If it wasn't for her dedication to take me to the training sessions every week, watch my games and support me, I don't know where I would be now. She has changed my life.

Prue also invites me and my sister to stay with her on regular occasions. She shares her life with us, tell us stories and makes us feel like family. I can honestly say that those stays are some of the highlights of the year.

Prue showed me that people can be kind, kind to strangers and kind to people who live a different life to them. She showed me that no matter where you live in the world, or where you have come from, it is the kindness of your neighbour and friends that make you feel at home.

Act 1

Margot Przymierska

Margot is an artist, writer and performer born in Bialystok, Poland. She came to UK in 2003.

It's not even a story, to be fair, just a normal kind of – Oops, I live here now, innit.

There's no reason really to even go there, 'cuz you ain't gonna find anything interesting. No reason, no drama, nothing worth mentioning in your Insta story. Maybe one day I'll make a TV show about it. It will go something like:

"Ladies, gentlemen, and other genders, welcome to the Great Migration Show, where Margot – formerly known as Małgorzata – reveals her reasons for leaving Poland."

Part 1: A Lesbian Affair.

Is it still a lesbian matter if the star of the show wasn't even sure if she liked girls in the first place? I mean, at 18 it's hard to be sure about anything, let alone things like a mega-crush on an androgynous-looking friend, who has left Białystok for England one day.

And BTW, don't try dissing the city of Białystok, yeah, cuz it's the main one there in the region mate. FYI, the one that hasn't been demoted in the great administrational conflict – The Reform – let's party like it's 1999, unlike other settlements scattered like crumbs, Białystok towering is loud and proud, so shut your mouth, just because you're living in the big London town doesn't mean you can cast judgements on geographic locations you simply know nothing about.

Anyway, as I was saying, what do you know about

yourself at 18? The rejections hurt. It was the first chance to take her life in her hands and leave Bialystok, (ain't nothing wrong with the place, y'hear!).

It was the first chance to take her life in her hands, unmitigated by her mentally ill mother and hardworking father. Oh, he was hardworking, alright, working hard to intimidate her sensitivity, sitting on the sofa in front of the TV, in his underwear, playing with his testicles – that's the level of mindless familiarity that is hard to bear for an artistic 18-year-old, let's face it, hardly inspiring sight, nothing to write home about.

The late night calls on the landline – the phone's cord stretched to its limits between the hall and the bedroom, sliding door shut, yet with huge gaps between the edge of the door and the carpeted floor (she didn't choose the colour) and the paper-thin walls of a 39m2 box in a social block studded with invigilante neighbours. Old women – dog walkers – whose antennae pick up the faintest whisper of softly unfolding blossom of the first serious conversation featuring feelings and attempts at naming the status quo between our star and the androgenous … lover (God, how things have moved on). Some words spoken out loud, ever so quietly, for the first time, micro-movements of hands, gazes over the first ever beer with raspberry syrup in a place where nobody asked for the IDs. It was nice that.

Until that old one with a mohair beret and a plastic bag scrunched up under her garb, stuffed with unidentified objects, what's that all about? How many times is it normal to circle the grass bit by the bins, like it's some kind of an outlet for existential first aid kits and past the sale by date sweets.

Paid advertisement starts here
The kits come in all shapes and sizes, for tears and general sadness, for marital infidelity and dogs swapped at birth …
Keep in rigid covers for maximum duration and personal satisfaction …
Sweets – a reminder that things could get harder, so appreciate what you've got …
Items for consumption at client's own risk …
Alternatively, they make original ornaments – perfect as birthday gifts …
Paid advertisement ends here

Until that one, the Bin Shopping Queen with meticulously applied lipstick pearly pink, with a fat dotted dog that was gonna be a miniature poodle but turned out to be a cheap Russian scam, much larger in fact than anticipated by anyone, most of all her.

The Human Bear, who once upon a time wished for a child, but the male rejection stuck in her heart like a shard, so, she settled for a cute pup. It could have been perfect but was swapped at birth or spent too much time amidst the ambiguous Western goods of compromised quality, brought to you painstakingly on a longer detour via Azerbaijan, Kazakhstan, deep taigas, tundras and meanders of the Eastern barons in charge to the town market underneath the arch. Truly international stuff.

Now, for the last time -

Things were going well until that old one, picked up the latest intel on the budding love, and released it to the aether guarded perversely by a whole army of them, some worse – more wrinkly and with uglier dogs. Rumours spread like wildfire, which engulfed both parents like a pair of potatoes thrown into the fire – essentially perfectly lovely when cooled down a tad. However, bursting with heat of wrath right now. Keep your distance! Good luck!

With only 39m2 worth of floor to move around, nowhere was far enough from the lava of accusations, overspill of expectations, family shame. And all she's been thinking about was how a man who spends his life between shifts, clad in a skimpy pair of briefs and a wife-beater, how does he get to call the shots? Talk about family shame, for real!

And her little cousin – camp as Christmas – will join the priesthood in a few years' time, raising zero suspicions amid uncles and aunts. How's that fair?

Speaking of queer raves, on 25th of December 2003, after three months of separation, letters sent across borders, our anti-hero here, enrols successfully onto a Polish Philology degree course – next best thing after an epic failure with the exam for the prestigious acting school in the capital – Damn them! Rigged, the whole thing anyway.

The process of "straightening" in the eyes of the parents went extremely well, so much so that the permit to visit her "friend" in England was granted in the shape of a coach ticket. Thirty-one hours from the departure she arrived at Victoria Coach Station. Free and terrified.

But don't panic, child, remember the training, the breathing, the spatial awareness. Take it all in. Your greatest acting challenge begins.

In this New Land I had Found a Lover

Hajra

> This piece reflects the sorrow of leaving your home
> country and the challenges of new experiences but
> gives hope that with time, you can make and love a
> new home.

No ship could encapsulate the feeling on leaving your
home,
travelling from one world into another, that you could
only now reach from a phone.
I remember the first day I came,
I had reached a land I didn't know I could ever claim.
I had walked down the new streets,
so far that I couldn't feel my feet.
It was a chilly day in spring,
and I sat in the park on a swing.
The leaves were slowly coming back to life,
and the smell of freshly cut grass was rife.
I looked at the lively city in front of me,
thinking about what my life would now be.
Now I sit in the exact same spot,
with three years of experience that I have now got.
I recall the moment very vividly,
when the sun had sat quietly.
The silence was loud,
and the moon shone proud.
I realised that I had now started to call this place home,
and I no longer felt alone.
I made new friends,
who were all gems.
I had left my home to find another,
and in this new land I had become a lover.

TGIUK

Migrating to the UK

Sumia

This writing shows how the environment in which we live can empower us and give us the strength to stand up for people who are not as fortunate. By migrating to the UK, Sumia has found her voice and is using it to protect others.

I am lucky; I was granted a visa to allow me to migrate to the UK. Living in the UK has given me opportunities and the confidence to not only speak for myself but also for those who are unable to speak up.

But first I want to tell you about myself and how I was as a young girl. I was very shy, feeble, and a highly sensitive person. I never stood up for my rights despite the many injustices I endured or witnessed. But growing up experiencing mistreatment and being neglected taught me an important lesson; if you don't stand up for yourself then don't expect it from anybody else.

And so, now I try to be as strong as I can. I have learnt to speak not for only my own sake but for that of all the Baloch community, especially for the hundreds of Baloch women who cannot speak up for their rights or their freedom.

The UK is a democratic country; it gives you your rights no matter where you are from or who you are. After I came to the UK, I became a stronger, more empowered person as I had the freedom to be the person I wanted to be. In the UK, I can achieve anything I set my mind to. Now I can freely speak up for myself and for my nation. I can freely introduce myself to anyone without restrictions. I feel more confident, and I feel more secure in this country and most importantly, I am free to choose any field of work or studies.

I am lucky; I was granted a visa to allow me to migrate to the UK.

Fly if you Can

Damayanthi Muthukumaranage

Damayanthi is a human-rights activist originally from
Sri Lanka, who continuously campaigns to promote
peace, gender equality, and women's rights. She is
currently living in the UK and working with the Arts
Council, England, on diversity and inclusion.

Break and throw
chains tied legs.
Come and walk
this new ground
without fear or suspicion.

Get on your feet.
Smile, fly if you can,
underneath this cold sky with no barriers.

Delicious food, colourful dresses.
Smiling faces,
hearts full of love.
Embrace with love.

In this path there is no fear or loneliness,
come and enjoy the life
while respecting diversity.

TGIUK

Musaab's Story

Musaab

Despite trauma, Musaab has never given up and considers himself 'lucky'. His story is one of hope and guidance to migrants newly arrived in the UK. Musaab's writing was edited to allow the reader to better understand his story, but it remains his voice and his story.

I've had many difficult days since I left my country, but I have never given up. I am still alive.

I lived in Libya in the most difficult days of torture, threats and exploitation that transformed the "cut of the sea from Europe" but I was lucky.

Lucky, I arrived in Europe, but life there was still difficult and while I felt safer than before, I didn't find stability. I was homeless and living on the streets. I was told the only place to find stability was to go to the United Kingdom.

I went through many traumas to get here, but eventually I arrived, and finally feel safe and stable. The difficulties I encountered are experienced by many of the migrants I speak with today. I try to guide them according to my experience.

To avoid becoming a stereotype, the "cliched" migrant, you must merge into your new culture. It is essential to understand and study your host country well. I think it is done most fully by two factors: language, and work. I believe that whoever, for whatever circumstances, migrants to Europe, must realise that it is not an easy dream. There are opportunities, but it takes intelligence and perseverance. I want any young person to know that, and to know that it is possible to succeed.

I set myself a goal and achieved it.

Achieving your goals is always possible. However, I also learned that there are obstacles that must be avoided to achieve your goals and live a decent life. It is the truth that illegal work, aid dependence, and state abuse are things that will not benefit any refugee in the long run. On the contrary … it may threaten your chance of staying in this country.

I am lucky, I made it out of Libya, and I have a new safe and stable life in the UK.

Lost or Found?

Thomas Spoelstra

Thomas was born in South Africa in 2008 and came to the UK as a four-year-old boy in 2012. His mother taught him basic English as soon as they arrived, and he improved his English-speaking skills watching lots of *Thomas the Tank Engine* and *Fireman Sam*. Thomas wrote this poem to share the experiences of a migrant child who faced a lot of discrimination and being questioned about who he was and how having a British passport was not enough to make him British in the eyes of his peers. He is proud to consider himself British.

Lost or found?
Should I respond to the droning of the South African drum?
I hear about your thunder; I see images of your lightning strikes over the bare ridden landscape ... wild animals roaming the bushveld.
Lost ...
I am given traditional food at home, listen to South African music, still speak my mother tongue Afrikaans – all to remind me of my heritage and country of birth.
Found ...
But I don't remember this place once called home. I can only relive some of it through your eyes - Mum and Dad – I remember grandad, but not his stories. They are not part of me anymore.
Lost ...
Nationally – British citizen. I know nothing else. Victoria Sponge, Bangers and Mash, Sunday Roast, Fish and Chips and Eton Mess. This is what I know best.
Found ...

Most tell me I don't belong, I'm not what my passport says. I'm not British because I was born in deep dark Africa. I have to explain in vain about this stain of legal immigration.

Lost ...

Family sacrifices made when I was four – I remember nothing about this detour. Leaving behind everything and everyone we knew, to open a new door.

Found ...

Great Britain – now a teenager – swearing allegiance to Queen and country. The only country I call home. The only place I've ever truly known.

Perhaps still stained. Lost ... Found.

My Journey

Liz Mingo

Liz was born in the Commonwealth of Dominica, West Indies. She came to England with her mother in January 1975. Her mother came to join her husband who she married in Dominica. He left for England, and they followed him later. The poem shows the confusion of arrival but also that life gets better.

Came here when I was 10 years old.
Often heard that the English streets were paved with gold!
Not quite sure I knew what that meant, in all honesty,
it's just something I kept hearing, constantly,
from elders, obviously.
I assumed they'd seen stories about England on TV.
But, guess as time approached,
I'd have the opportunity
to see with my own eyes.
And when we arrived in January 1975 - "permission to swear?"
nothing but white, fluffy stuff everywhere!
"What the..."
This must be the gold I kept hearing about!
This must be it; this must be gold.
It has to be, cause I can't see the road.
But no-one said that gold was cold!
We arrived at our address in NW10.
This was home, where we'd be staying.
When my stepfather opened the door,
yummy smells were coming from the kitchen.
Thought he'd laid on a feast for us,
but when I walked in, my face dropped!
Strangers! Who were this couple?

If I'd spoken, it wouldn't have been subtle,
so, I said nothing!
We walked into a tiny room, which only had one bed,
then realisation hit!
This wasn't just our house.
Turns out,
we were all in the same boat.
The kitchen, bathroom and toilet had to be shared.
I became more of an introvert!
We did eventually find our own place
and I welcomed my own room and much more space!
Many, many years have since passed - 46 to be exact,
but when I look back,
I'd be lying if I said it didn't get a whole lot better.
And not sure I'd want to change any of it either!
But sadly, I lost my mother in 1984.
Hadn't experienced that kind of pain before.
I'd lost family members of course,
But mum and me were tight!
Most times it was just the two of us.
I've been back to the Caribbean many times.
And it's an important journey to make.
It helps me appreciate
all I've gained,
since migrating to England!
This journey has played a big hand
in who I am today!
I have an open mind.
Yes, I left family and friends behind, but what I've
gained is so much more.
Coming here opened many a door!
And I'm doing things I truly adore - writing, playing
sports, visiting the theatre.
England offers an array of things to do and explore!
Dominica will forever be in my heart, my soul, my blood,

because it is where I was born!
But, arriving here in 1975, when I made my journey,
doors were truly opened for ME!
I say it sometimes, albeit quietly,
but now it's on paper, for all to see - thank you, ENGLAND!
Your streets were never paved with gold,
and I'm all too familiar with the cold!
But small fish I say,
'cause the advantages far out way!
The only negative to this narrative
and my only alteration to this script
is that mum would be here, to see and read this
masterpiece!
Thank you for allowing me
the opportunity
to share my story!

TGIUK

CHAPTER 5 - RELATIONSHIP WITH COUNTRY OF ORIGIN

Dr Alexandra Bulat

Dr Alexandra Bulat is a migration researcher and migrants' rights campaigner. She was awarded a PhD in Political Sociology and Migration Studies from UCL in 2020 and co-manages the youth wing of the citizens' rights organisation, the3million, the Young Europeans Network. Alexandra was elected in May 2021 as the first Romanian Labour County Councillor, representing the Abbey division in Cambridgeshire.

To understand migrants' lives in the United Kingdom, it's essential to recognise and respect the complex relationship migrants have with their country of origin. As such, I am pleased to introduce this chapter reflecting that special connection migrants have with their countries of origin. I believe that the strong connection that many migrants hold with the countries they were born and usually grew up in enhances their experiences and the social, economic, cultural, and political contributions they make while living in the United Kingdom.

Often there is a perception that to be accepted here, migrants need to shed their home culture and traditions and disappear into a cloak of "Britishness". The reality is that experiencing different cultures empowers us to be more open, accepting, and welcoming of other people. As one of our writers beautifully underlined, *"I won't erase a culture of my own".*

Migration is not a new phenomenon in the UK, and we cannot underestimate its positive impacts throughout history. I am proud to be British-Romanian

– I naturalised as a British citizen because the UK is my home, but this does not mean my Romanian roots are not important. I will always say I am the first Romanian-born county councillor. Having lived experience as a migrant adds value to the work I do in politics and in the public sector. Speaking about our ethnicity can positively influence and shape other people's attitudes to those they consider different.

Before the EU referendum in 2016, I was not involved in migrants' rights campaigning. Migrant voices were rarely heard, and this motivated me to get active, first volunteering and then working for the3million. Organisations such as TogetherintheUK (TGIUK) provide a safe platform for migrants' voices to be heard and be respected – I am delighted to support this initiative.

Long Distance Relationship

Meduulla

Meduulla was born in Zimbabwe and moved to the UK when she was three years old. She wrote the poem during her second year of university, where she first began to explore her identity as a first-generation immigrant. This prize-winning poem helped her embrace and love her unique heritage that combines Zimbabwean and British culture.

There are oceans and seas that stand between you and me,
and the story of our love is an old forgotten odyssey.
And I know it's odd to see me being held by him,
be encompassed by a new set of arms. I feel like I'm forgetting the shade of those ruddy red palms and that deep, drumming voice, religiously reciting foreign psalms.
Your heart, radiated a heat that hugged and honed my youthful body, and I never quite understood why your voice rushed when reading, or why psalms sounded sorrowful,
but it was because you knew, I wouldn't last long in your arms.
Being with you was like loving someone who only kissed me in public, you wore your name on my passport for the world to see,
but behind closed colonial doors,
we were strangers.
That was the danger of long-distance relationships,
we had latitudes of land in between us, and the lies of our love had been left to marinade for too long.
You see, I had heard of you, but only through televisions

that told tall tales of your tribulations,
I was taught that I had to leave you if I had any chance
of an education,
that you were no good for me, and I should feel nothing
but gratification.
It's been 18 years since I left you,
18 years that I've been calling for your rescue,
so for those 18 years, I had to find a place of refuge.
But now he who holds me hates me, sells me dwindled
dreams of democracy,
I see that he's looking at me through his colour-blind
prism, which is why he doesn't understand when I speak
to him of isms,
because my native tongue is a self-conflicting prison.
He who holds me, prays for our continued separation,
he laughs at my inability to say no more than 'wuri sayi'
as a form of feeble communication,
it's like I'm watching myself, losing myself but I'm still
struggling to change the station.
The murmurs about my motherland have turned into
echoes in my eardrum,
I have lost home in this not so United Kingdom.
This must be what they call Stockholm Syndrome
because I had fallen in love with my abductor,
the reason, and the remedy for my Rhodesian rupture.
And I knew this, but I still called him home.
You my home, and him my harbour, have a complex
history, so I have to choose,
I have to choose between the love I have now, and love
I once knew,
but if home is where the heart is, my heart resides with
you.
We encountered each other again,
and only then did I understand why the fruits of your
labour tasted so bitter.

We were by the Zambezi River,
I told you about how my lip quivers each time I utter a
word in my mother tongue ...
but I'd rather stutter and stammer your sentence, than
speak his English with ease.

TGIUK

An Old Newspaper

Susan Ozer

> Dr Susan Ozer came to the UK in 1995, having finished her medical degree and her initial training in Ghana. She wrote this prize-winning story for her mama, whom she admires greatly. She also wanted to share her parents' story with other readers, hoping that they would enjoy reading it as much as she had writing it.

Nesting in a warm fluid of love with a heartbeat so strong it lulls me to sleep. I feel heat and recoil at once further into my warm fluid chamber. I taste the food she eats; the drink she drinks and wonder how she knows what makes me tick. I hear every night the music she plays, muffled laughter, voices, dances and jumps that makes me kick.

On a warm summer's day, I hear the long blast of a horn, quarrelsome sea gulls, distant chimes, and sense a pulling away from a cherished island. Mama though is happy about something, she keeps bringing up fluid, making me squirm and twist in my warm and comfy home, filled with love so strong it blinds.

Whoa ... I sense sudden heat, temperature change, but wait a minute, so much laughter, so much love, and then all this sudden rush of heady endorphins through the cord that binds. I wonder where Mama is right now, the food she eats, movements she makes catapulting me into dreamless sleeps.

Fast forward 50+3 years or more – I see a tattered photo of her, a newspaper print brown and yellow with age, hid in a dark corner for years and years and smells like ancient sage. There she is, my mama dearest, with a bump that is me, stepped off a ship sailed for weeks on deep blue sea. Mama may be in in her twenties or maybe more, and beautiful as I imagined her to be, with almondy brown eyes, velvety smooth skin, medium dark hair tied back with something that spells 'P'. I see my mama in this old and tattered newspaper print, on that day 50+3 years or more ago and the feelings that I felt – the pictures in my developing brain of firing synaptic neurones, a tiny baby growing in mama's womb – exactly how I imagined her to be.

She has travelled from England with dad to a land they used to call Gold Coast, hope, and pride, daddy standing proudly by her side. Mama is surrounded by family and warmth and to cries of 'Akwaba ooo', which means in Ghanaian 'welcome, welcome'- daddy standing proudly by her side.

I can now see 50+3 years or more what was on the outside through a tattered newspaper print - a photo, faded, yellow with age and smelling like ancient sage, a precious glimpse of me in mama's bump, stepped off a big ship christened Rift, a beautiful treasure so hard to find, no ultrasound photos in those days – so please be kind.

I am now back in this beautiful green country called England, where my life literally begun, 25+ years or more to date. The people, accents, food, smells, the music of the sixties that makes me cry and brings up memories of mum and dad and still do not know why.

Like mama, I have grown to love this island, otherwise why does my heart jump when the plane emerges from the clouds, and see the land spread out right in front of my eyes?

I know that mama dear is proud of that little bump. I have grown to be in this England, a front-line health worker, just like mama was, serving in one of the greatest institutions in the world. I am now 50+3 years and more to date, and know mama, will definitely agree.

British Punjabi

Goody

Goody's father came to the UK in 1956 as an 18-year-old immigrant from the Punjab in India. Her mother came six years later. Goody was born in Leeds in 1967 and lived in a diverse community with immigrants from the Punjab, Jamaica, Pakistan Poland, and Ireland, who all supported each other. Her parents spoke their native language and Goody and her twin brothers grew up speaking both Punjabi and English fluently. Goody is proud of her heritage and wrote this poem for her father, who died in 2002 and for her mother, who at 82, still lives in Leeds.

I am a second-generation Punjabi.
I won't be a clone
I won't erase a culture of my own.
Alongside being British,
I won't take the Punjab
out of my bones.
The land my mother and father loved,
as well as Britain.
When people say
'Speak English'
I proudly say, 'This is my language too,
I can speak two'.
I won't extinguish Punjabi,
the language I learnt
before English,
my mother tongue.
The language which allows me to converse
with so many wonderful people
when I visit the Punjab

and the Punjabi elders there.
I won't put it in a hearse,
I will always embrace
the heritage that runs through me,
like the five rivers of the Punjab.

Growing up "Different" to my Mum

Erica Pham

> Erica's mother is from Vietnam, and spent some time in Hong Kong. Erica's family came to the UK when she was two. Erica and her mother only speak to each other in Cantonese, their second language, and so there has often been miscommunication between the two. Erica believes that rather than being a challenge, this dynamic makes life both unique and always interesting.

Born in Hong Kong but raised in England.
It was a big change, but I knew no different.
You see, my parents just wanted something different, something more.
I understand it so much better now, than I ever did before.
I never even knew I was "different" until people would tell me "It's a cold sore"– not "coleslaw". It's "switch off the light" not "close the light".

To think I grew up only speaking one language and now I think in another.
To think I grew up speaking one language to parents but another to my sister and brother.
Oh, the loss of cultural identity. That was hard for my mother.

Cultural identity. It runs deeper than mere speech and language.
It's being proud of who you are, but I grew up feeling different and ashamed and it caused my mother so much anguish.

High school was difficult, I just wanted to be like my friends.
I felt she didn't understand me, we would drive each other round the bend.
I would say "why don't you show me physical affection; like the mothers of my friends?"
It must have made her feel terrible, but she knew there was a positive end.
"Baby, don't you understand, I don't need to give you cuddles to show I love you" in other words "please understand, that I work so tirelessly so that you can do whatever you want to".

And now I am living my best life and I am the happiest I have ever been.
My mum went through tough times to get here, to support me, make me independent so that I can live my dream.
You see, she was so selfless that she never expected affection or love back from her children.
Her sole purpose as a mother was to provide them with everything they could have ever needed.

Now I am proud of who I am and my cultural identity.
I understand that this parenting is what was best for me.

I could have never done half the things I have done if it wasn't for the bravery of my mum.

Holland my Home

Mark Fairweather

Mark though English, grew up in Holland, a country
which he considers his true home. He moved to the
UK with his father who was taking up a new job in
the UK. His poem gives the reader insight into the
love many children have for the country in which
they grew up and reflects the bittersweet emotions
of migrants as they adapt to their new home.

When I lived in Holland
I learnt Dutch
I spoke it well
And enjoyed it so much

At school I spoke English
And it was a blast
I was at that school
What felt like forever

I still do remember
What happened day in day out
The teachers who taught me
And friends I hung around

I do wish I could go back there
I consider it a home to me
A place to recall
Long forgotten memories

It's true, I'm English but what does it matter
After eleven years, this is where I grew up
A place with no hills

And food so tasty, it will sweep you off your feet

Holland has its traditions
Just like Saint Nick
He goes by Sinterklaas
With his helper Zwarte Piet
Sinterklass rode a horse pure white in colour
And during the night Zwarete Piet comes down
Everyone's chimneys in all of the houses laying gifts of
plenty in clogs or shoes

It's truer than ever just how much I retain
All the stuff I remember rattling in my brain
The mouth-watering confectionary
Yes, I still recall the food and the drink
Holland is my home and the place I grew up

Fighting with my Conscience

Althia Anson-Barnett

Althia was born in Jamaica and migrated to the UK in 2002. She was motivated to write when she joined a writing group in Birmingham. She had some training in journalism before the pandemic started in 2020. The group became a lifeline for her during lockdown imposed during the COVID pandemic.

Where I am from is bright and sunny,
I have an intention … the intention to go somewhere far.
But am fighting with my conscience, I have no money.
The idea keeps nagging and nagging in my head,
Oh my God, my children need schooling … I know, I know! They must be fed.
I do not know how long the journey will take. My children are left with older siblings and
my family with the tasks. All for love's sake.
I want to turn back when I see the big shiny bird …
but the feeling of trepidation would not allow me to utter a word.
Hoping against hope, I continue with my journey,
as the desire of new life in a new world beckon. The thought of earning money.
I get to the end and begin to weep …
I weep for my children and for my life. When darkness falls and the night is silent,
I put my head down and I cannot go to sleep.
The thoughts of my homeland and love filled years of what I left behind,
the effortless tears flood my eyes and I'm filled with fears.

All these thoughts keep going around and around in my mind,
not knowing if what I came in search of, I'll ever find.

Homeland

Jaimin

This is Jaimin's second poem, and it continues his theme of exploring what it means to move from your home country and to understand what or where home is. And it reflects the importance of having a community which links to your culture.

By plane we came, to a new life.
I learnt the new language.
I learnt the new culture.
I learnt the new system.

I can greet people.
I can manage the papers.
I can drop my children to school.

I can work.
I can cook food.
I can fix the car when it breaks down.

I know these things.
I learn these things.
I fit into these things.

But, at home when my work is done,
there is not a single thing, that is more wholesome,
nor more fulfilling, than being able to talk,
with my brother, sister, mother, father, son, daughter,
my family, and all my friends, closest to my heart,
who have seen the sun depart, in all its hues,
in our old land, in the tongue our ancestors gave,
as we laugh, eat, and drink, freely, in our new walls,
that is now our home.

TGIUK

EDITOR'S BIOGRAPHIES

Teresa Norman

This anthology feels to me like a culmination of so much of my working and academic life. In the 1980s, I studied English Literature at St. Andrews. I gained insight into how literature helps you live, through giving you insight. It also taught me how to create a structure that tells a story.

For over ten years, I have worked in diversity – this has made me aware of the importance of hearing different voices and creating a platform for those voices. This is what the Anthology has done. I believe my talent to be an unusual one, it is to facilitate the talent of others. I am proud of the creativity, quirkiness and literary quality of the authors in the book and that I have played a role in bringing them to publication.

TGIUK

Sinéad Mangan-Mc Hale

Working in the corporate world as both a writer and an editor, I communicate the pros and cons of energy, real estate, financial planning, and so many more diverse commercial products and services, but working on this anthology gave me the greatest joy. Volunteering with TogetherintheUK enables me to use my writing skills to share migrant and refugee stories to show that we all have the same hopes and dreams for ourselves and our families.

As an editor, my role is not to rewrite but rather to enhance the story; to bring an extra layer of depth to the stories the author is conveying. Against all my professional training, in this anthology, I have left much of the writing as the authors intended; with grammatical errors ignored as we, TogetherintheUK and Victorina Press, sought to share the stark honesty of the authors' stories. To edit their words would have been to rewrite their experiences, to disguise their pain, sorrow, loneliness, hope, joy, or the discrimination they face. We want and need you, the reader, to hear their stories as they told them and lived them.

As a migrant myself, the stories resonated deeply with me. I did not experience a dangerous, abusive journey, but the sadness of leaving my family remains in my heart even after many years. We may never resolve the causes behind the rise of refugees and migrants, but we can always offer a smile and words of encouragement to those we meet.

Consuelo Rivera-Fuentes

The publishing world, artificially, divides books into fiction and non-fiction. But for me, all literary genres use strategies to express truths and realities of human, animal and environmental nature. The spider's web which makes us co-evolve as we read and write has, since childhood, wrapped me with strong threads which have dressed my travels. In 2017 I embarked on a new cobbled path of books when I founded the publishing house Victorina Press, which is named after my mother. This new journey – like all others I have done as a teacher, writer, and editor – is strongly rooted in Pachamama and in Chile, my motherland, where volcanoes throw ardent kisses to rivers, mountains, deserts, seas, and forests.

I am an academic, but I like that public space of loitering where I can unleash my creativity. I have been part of several creative writing groups because I like to read, write and 'to memory' in solidarity and accompanied, although I also give myself time to be alone with myself. This has resulted in several books of poetry and narrative. In my books of poetry entitled *La*

Liberación de la Eva Desgarrada (1990) and *Arena en la Garganta* (2010) I try to face that grit that scrapes my throat and my voice when I tell in metaphors what happens through my body now, during and after the torture to which I was subjected in Chile in 1983.

TogetherintheUK, along with Victorina Press, hope that you enjoyed reading these beautiful stories and poems. To read similar stories and to connect with migrants and refugees, please visit our website www.togetherintheuk. co.uk and follow us on Instagram @togetherintheuk, Twitter @TogetherintheUK, Facebook @Together In The UK – TGIUK, LinkedIn @TogetherintheUK
www.victorinapress.com

TGIUK